DREAMING AS ONE

Poetry, Poets and Community in Bolinas, California, 1967-1980

Kevin Opstedal

ISBN: 979-8-9894133-8-6

This book was first published in the online journal *Big Bridge* (edited by Michael Rothenberg) in 2008.

Grateful acknowledgement is made to RiskPress Foundation for making The Divers Collection possible.

"Dreaming As One / for Tom & Angelica" is the title of a poem by Lewis Warsh and was used as the title of a book of his poetry published by Corinth Books in 1971. "Dreaming As One" is also the title of a song written by David Palmer and William Smith, and first recorded in 1975 by Jackie De Shannon.

Cover photo of Bill Berkson, Lewis Warsh, Joanne Kyger, and Andre Codrescu on the steps of the Waring House, Bolinas, 1970, by Elizabeth Leon Kirkland.
Back cover image by Ronan Furuta.

Author Photo by Pamela Dewey

fmsbw

San Francisco, California

This is Bolinas, California.
The home of the poets.

— Aram Saroyan

PREFACE

I started this project in 1985. By 2006 I had a draft ready and sent it to Joanne Kyger, Lewis MacAdams, Bill Berkson, and Duncan McNaughton for approval. They all made useful suggestions and were very enthusiastic about the book. When I had it all fixed up, I sent it to several potential publishers. Everyone passed on it. In 2008 Joanne told Michael Rothenberg about the book, and he contacted me with the idea of publishing the whole thing in his online literary journal *Big Bridge*. Since it didn't seem likely that I'd find a publisher anytime soon, I agreed.

Because nothing very substantial had been written about the Bolinas poetry scene of the 1970s previously, this work has been cited in many books and periodicals, including recently *The New Yorker*. While I am grateful for the acknowledgement, not for myself but for the poets I wrote about, there continue to be misconceptions. You'll find essays in print and online that claim Bolinas at that time was a town that was "run by the poets". That is incorrect. The poets in Bolinas during the 1970s were by no means "in charge". As I try to make clear in this book, Bolinas was a community that *included* poets. That is what made that place and time so remarkable.

I was fortunate enough to become close friends with many of the poets I interviewed for this book. We collaborated on many projects together, but just to talk, hang out, and read side-by-side at venues in San Francisco, Los Angeles, Boulder, and New York is something that I will always treasure. Although I had been thoroughly engaged in studying and writing poetry since high school, I had never been in contact with any poets until I started this project in 1985. These poets confirmed my calling, and sadly, not many are still with us.

It is to those who are gone and to those who are still here that I dedicate this book.

Kevin Opstedal
Santa Cruz, CA

INTRODUCTION
BOLINAS 2 MILES

It's easy to miss the turn-off. The road isn't marked. You've just driven north through the little town of Stinson Beach. Two-lane Highway 1 snakes between the edges of steep hills and arroyos on the right and a wide flat lagoon on the left. It's a winding corridor lined with eucalyptus, oak, willow, pine and alder trees. The lagoon, a mudflat at low tide, where egrets and herons hunt, and seals bask in the sunlight. As you drive past the lagoon there's a road to the left nearly hidden by dense trees and shrubs. You make that sharp left turn and another left, drive another mile or so on a straightaway beneath a canopy of eucalyptus, past an old-time country schoolhouse, until you see the street-sign for Mesa Road. Turning right you drive uphill through more eucalyptus, past a house or two just off the road. Near the top of the climb at Overlook Drive, you turn left. You are now on the Bolinas mesa.

One of the first things one might hear about Bolinas is the missing road sign. It is legendary. Sometime in the early 1970s, no one seems to know exactly when, the sign disappeared. Caltrans replaced the sign, and it promptly disappeared once again. Actually, the sign didn't "disappear", it was removed. This disappearing act was often attributed to the Bolinas Border Patrol, a shadowy ad hoc guerrilla organization which, depending on who you talk to, either does or doesn't exist. Caltrans continued to replace the "Bolinas 2 Miles" sign on a fairly regular basis into the 1980s. The Bolinas Border Patrol dutifully removed the sign each time. Finally, Caltrans just gave up.

On the mesa lies a grid of roads, most of them unpaved. Nestled in among the cypress, coyote brush and eucalyptus are houses—better described as cottages or bungalows, some no more than shacks, some prefab A-frames, or geodesic domes, while others are rustic wooden structures that seem to be a cross between a ranch-style tract home, a TV western set, and a Nantucket bed and breakfast. Various cars, trucks and vans parked along the road or in driveways run the gamut from rusted-out vintage VWs, late model pick-ups, and spanking new SUVs. As you drive along you catch a glimpse of a bumper sticker on one beat-up white Toyota pick-up parked on the side of the road. The bumper sticker reads "Bolinas Border Patrol".

You get out of the car and look around. It was here, on the Bolinas mesa, that a remarkable number of important American poets made their home during the 1970s. Why were these poets—which together represent a solid core sample of the avant-garde poets of the time—drawn to this remote little California coastal village? It was, and is, a beautiful spot. The rural setting of the mesa, the little downtown area on Wharf Road, the lagoon, the beach—Bolinas is a special place and in itself is as significant a character in this story as anyone who lived there.

Along with the important contingent of American poets that gathered in Bolinas at that time was also a varied group of psychedelic refugees, radical representatives of the sixties counterculture, artists, writers and visionaries. Together they created a community that was as unique and eclectic as were these individuals themselves.

BEGINNINGS

Bolinas sits on the ground
by the sea, sky
overhead.
                    - Robert Creeley

Perched upon the southernmost tip of the Point Reyes Peninsula, with the Pacific Ocean to the west and Bolinas lagoon to the east, the town of Bolinas seems like an island just offshore. One day it may be just that. Bolinas sits on the western side of the San Andreas Fault, the Pacific Plate, which is slowly pulling away from the continent. This geological fact is oddly in synch with the nature of the Bolinas citizenry who have worked so hard for so many years to keep the rest of the world at a distance. Despite its physical remoteness, and the prevailing isolationist attitude of its inhabitants, Bolinas wasn't always known as a place that discouraged visitors. The California Gold Rush of 1849 drew thousands of people from all over the world to San Francisco. Local entrepreneurs saw a chance to make their fortunes by filling the need for food and shelter for this tidal wave of immigrants. The land around Bolinas lagoon, about 30 miles north of San Francisco, was densely forested with redwood, oak and fir. Easily accessible by sea, boats could be loaded with lumber and other goods in Bolinas lagoon and ferried back down through the Golden Gate.

The boom that took place in San Francisco initiated a boom in Bolinas, which at that time encompassed a large swath of Marin County coastline, from Dogtown in the north to Stinson in the south—a parcel that had been part of a Mexican land grant to the Briones family. Sawmills sprang up overnight and Bolinas became a busy port city. Many ship captains and crew members also took up ranching and farming, producing goods for the San Francisco market. There were shipbuilding yards around the lagoon. Hotels and saloons sprang up along Wharf Road in Bolinas.

But by the late 1800s the silt build-up in the lagoon forced the ship builders to move elsewhere. It also made it impossible to use the lagoon as a port for supply ships to load their goods. The boom eventually went bust. Fishing, farming and ranching still went on there over the years, but Bolinas became more of a quiet, rural outpost than the bustling center of commerce it was during the boom years.

‡

By the 1960s Bolinas was a forgotten, scruffy little rural coastal town. Being just an hour north of San Francisco made it attractive as a getaway place for weekenders. Some, like San Francisco Chronicle feature writer Margot Doss and her husband, Kaiser physician John Doss, bought a second house there—in their case, a house that would serve as an entry point to many of the poets that eventually made Bolinas their home.

Bolinas was quiet, picturesque, and off the beaten path. Most of the weekend and summer beach goers chose Stinson Beach as their regular destination. A few surfers would hit Bolinas, but the place wasn't a heavy draw for tourists.

Just down the road, Stinson Beach had poetry connections to the 1950s North Beach scene in San Francisco. Poet Robert Duncan and artist Jess Collins had a house there, where poet Jack Spicer sometimes visited. Joanne Kyger among others participated in Duncan's poetry workshops held there. Later, in the mid-sixties, poets Lawrence Kearney and Richard Duerden were living in Stinson as well. Poet Philip Whalen lived for a short time in Duerden's garage.

In 1965 the writer Bill Brown, who had been living in Point Richmond in the East Bay, bought a parcel of land in Bolinas. Poet Jim Koller and Brown's son Tony were among those that helped clear the land, and a local Bolinas carpenter named Calagy Jones built the Brown's a house there.

Brown and Koller were the editors of the influential *Coyote's Journal*, a literary magazine which was started in 1964 by Koller and Ed Van Aelstyn. Van Aelstyn was previously the editor of *The Northwest Review*, a literary magazine published by the University of Oregon. The University suspended publication of the review in 1964 in reaction to an issue which contained work by Artaud, Whalen, and an interview with Fidel Castro. Koller, Van Aelstyn, and Will Wroth decided to start their own magazine, and *Coyote's Journal* was born. The journal printed an impressive array of poets and writers including Gary Snyder, Robert Duncan, Paul Blackburn, Charles Olson, Joanne Kyger, Allen Ginsberg, Richard Brautigan, Clark Coolidge, Larry Eigner, Anselm Hollo, Richard Duerden, Tom Pickard, Philip Whalen, and others. Coyote's Books had an equally impressive list of titles, including Charles Olson's *Reading At Berkeley*, Philip Whalen's *Every Day*, *Highgrade* and *You Didn't Even Try*, Allen Ginsberg's *Wichita Vortex Sutra*, and Michael McClure's controversial play *The Beard*. Many of these books were designed by Zoe Brown (who also designed and typeset books for Donald Allen's Grey Fox and Four Seasons Foundation books).

Brown's house on the Bolinas mesa had three bedrooms upstairs, a darkroom for Zoe, and downstairs, Brown's workspace for writing. The big kitchen area and living room were the center of activity. Koller built a loft over the carport where he stayed for a brief period before moving to nearby Sebastopol. Several of Brown and Koller's friends, mostly writers from San Francisco, made the trek north to visit and spend time with them in Bolinas. Among these were poets Lew Welch, Gary Snyder, Kirby Doyle, Philip Whalen, Joanne Kyger, and Richard Brautigan. Brautigan began writing his novel *In Watermelon Sugar* (which was published in 1968) while staying with a mutual friend near the Browns home in Bolinas.

Bill Brown was born in Seattle in 1918, had served in the Merchant Marines, in the British Ambulance Corps in North Africa, and then in the U.S. Infantry. He had survived the Italian campaign in World War II, but was captured by the Germans near Nancy, France, spending a year in a POW concentration camp in Poland before being freed by the Russians. His experiences as a POW are recounted in his novel *The Way to the Uncle Sam Hotel* (Coyote Books,1966).

Brown made his living in east Marin running a landscaping business. When Swiss-Italian poet Franco Beltrametti first came to the US from Japan in 1967, Philip Whalen, who was then in Kyoto, asked Koller to meet Beltrametti and his family at the pier, and drive with them to Bolinas. There Franco, his wife Judy, and their son Giona, were introduced to the Browns, Joanne Kyger, and Jack Boyce. Beltrametti returned to Bolinas in 1974, spending several months there.

Just north of Olema, between Point Reyes and Bolinas, Peter Coyote lived with a mix of truck people and Diggers, a notorious group of San Francisco anarchist street theater activists that promulgated counterculture ideals. Many of the group's members partied with the Browns in Bolinas.

‡

Another interesting person in Bolinas, one with heavy-duty Beat credentials, was Hal Chase. Originally from Denver, Colorado, Chase was pals with Neal Cassady and later attended Columbia University where he met Jack Kerouac. It was Chase who introduced Cassady to Kerouac and Ginsberg in 1946. The character named Chad King in *On the Road* is a thinly disguised Hal Chase.

In Bolinas Chase worked primarily as a boat-builder and was something of a visionary, preaching a return to nature, farming the land, and using local woods to make small fishing boats.

By 1968, there was an interesting mix forming in Bolinas, including both the older representatives of the San Francisco beat scene, and the younger hippies—representing two generations that shared a similar bohemian anarchist philosophy. Along with these newcomers were the long-time residents of Bolinas, mostly farmers and some fishermen. It was by all accounts a mellow scene, but there was revolution in the air.

‡

It's important here to understand the historical and cultural context. In the 1960s, America's materialism, as well as the country's cultural and political norms, were being questioned by a new counterculture of young people, generally referred to as hippies. It was a tumultuous time. By the late sixties controversial issues such as civil rights, the Vietnam War, nuclear arms, the environment, drug use, sexual freedom, and nonconformity were rallying points for the young whose lifestyle integrated ideals of peace, love, harmony, music, mysticism, and religions outside the Judeo-Christian tradition. Yoga, meditation, and psychedelic drugs were embraced as methods to expand individual (and collective) consciousness.

In 1967 the Human Be-In at San Francisco's Golden Gate Park attracted thousands and was a precursor to The Summer of Love. Among those taking part in the Be-In were counterculture luminaries Timothy Leary, Richard Alpert, Allen Ginsberg and Gary Snyder. People were encouraged to question authority in regard to the Vietnam war, civil rights, and women's rights.

Members of the counterculture believed their way of life should express their political and social beliefs. Personal appearance, song lyrics, and the arts were used to make both individual and communal statements. At the same time the counterculture shaped its own alternative media of underground newspapers and radio stations.

As the sixties wound down many within the counterculture dropped out and left the cities for the countryside to experiment with utopian lifestyles. Away from urban problems and suburban sameness, they built new lives structured around shared political goals, organic farming, community service, and the longing to live simply with one's peers.

In San Francisco the blissful 3-month dream known as The Summer of Love had shattered into police shakedowns and drug busts. Predatory rip-offs of the spaced-out youth that flocked to the city were rampant. Bolinas was one place you could go to get away from the street hassles and into the back-to-nature bio-ethos that was a hippie ideal. The proximity to San Francisco, as well as the rugged beauty and rural setting made the place a primo find.

Not to be discounted as one of the attractive features of the town was the fact that Bolinas was (and still is) an unincorporated municipality—no city government, no police force. The downtown area consisted of about 2 blocks on Wharf Road. Smiley's Bar,

Scowley's Cafe, and Pepper's (the general store) were the highlights. To the north of downtown, up on the mesa, was a scattering of rough little cottages settled in among eucalyptus, cypress, and Monterey pines. Giant cascades of nasturtiums spilling over wooden fences. From the mesa bluffs, towering over Duxbury Reef, the largest shale reef in North America, you could hear the tide movements carried up on the almost constant sea breeze.

A TOTALLY SYMBOLIC LOCATION

In the late sixties Bolinas was still more of a place to get away to from the city than an ultimate destination. In 1968 poet Tom Clark's ultimate destination was San Francisco. Born in Oak Park, Illinois, in 1941, Clark had relocated to New York City in the late sixties after spending two years in England on a Fulbright scholarship. While in England he landed the position of poetry editor on *The Paris Review*. It was in this capacity that he began to form what would turn out to be important friendships with the young poets who were often referred to as members of the Second Generation New York School—poets such as Ron Padgett, Bill Berkson, Lewis Warsh, Anne Waldman, Dick Gallup, and Ted Berrigan. Living in New York provided an opportunity to be in close contact with these poets on a daily basis and take part in the vibrant poetry community on the lower east side.

Shortly after marrying Angelica Heinegg in 1968, Clark decided to make his way to the west coast. The newlyweds were joined by poet Lewis MacAdams and his wife Phoebe on a cross country drive to San Francisco. They were drawn by The Summer of Love and the underground scene there as portrayed in such publications as the wildly psychedelic *San Francisco Oracle*. As MacAdams recalled, "We read this psychedelic paper, the *Oracle*, with all these colors jumping out of it, and we said, fuck, man, let's move to San Francisco!"

The journey west was interrupted by a car wreck in Ohio. The Volvo driven by Phoebe had a blow-out at seventy miles-per-hour and rolled across the turnpike. Clark broke his collarbone but no one else was seriously injured. The trip continued via train to Denver where MacAdams got the news that the draft board in Texas was calling him. He and Phoebe headed to Dallas to deal with that, while the Clarks hopped on a plane to San Francisco. They were met at the airport by poet Joanne Kyger and her husband, the painter, Jack Boyce. Since Clark was still experiencing considerable discomfort from his broken collarbone, Kyger and Boyce summoned John Doss to have a look at him. After examining Clark, Doss advised, "Go with the pain".

The Clarks found that the rosy picture of a thriving hippie paradise in San Francisco, conjured by reports of the Summer of Love, was sadly no longer real. The Haight was full of burn-outs, cops were everywhere, and there was no place to hide.

At the suggestion of poet David Schaff, the Clarks headed up to Bolinas. They were just looking for a place to lay out for a while, but the beauty of Bolinas hooked them immediately. Compared to the lower east side of New York, and the Haight in San Francisco, Bolinas was Paradise. John and Margot Doss graciously offered to let the Clarks stay in their Bolinas vacation house while they searched for a place of their own. Shortly thereafter they found a small house on the mesa above Agate Beach, situated at the corner of Nymph and Cherry Roads. "It seemed like a totally symbolic location," said Clark.

Angelica was pregnant.

‡

One poet already in the Bolinas when the Clarks arrived was John Thorpe. The son of a Princeton professor, who later became the curator of the Huntington Library, Thorpe was briefly enrolled at Princeton. It was there that he met another future poet, Lewis MacAdams, who would also live for a considerable length of time in Bolinas. As MacAdams recalls, the floor of Thorpe's dorm room at Princeton was covered in dirt, soil, with which he was attempting to cultivate an experimental indoor garden.

Thorpe was known to most people in Bolinas as Shao, a name that was given to him by one of his professors at Princeton. "Shao" in Chinese means young, or new. As Tom Clark said, "I never heard a person in town call him John or Thorpe. To the outside world he was John Thorpe, in Bolinas it was Shao." Shao has been characterized by Clark as the poetic spirit of the town, "like a pixie spirit—he had a big friendly paleolithic beard and would reel about the mesa in the middle of the night to be found in a ditch with a bottle of wine at 3:00 a.m. staring at the stars."

While this characterization may hold some truth, it distracts from the fact that Thorpe was, and is, a powerful poet. "Shao's learning is incredible," said MacAdams, "God knows what he thinks of his own poetry, but to me he is the true poet of Bolinas."

Thorpe lived in the most amazing circumstances with his wife Renee and their children, the house teeming with rabbits, chickens, children, dogs, etc. "He told me," MacAdams recalls, "that the reason he wound up in Bolinas was because the welfare benefits were better in Marin County than they were in San Francisco." Kyger remembered that Renee's practicality really held things together. She knew how to work the welfare system and keep things afloat. Thorpe found odd jobs around town from time to time, did some farming, hustled up what money he could, and continued his own intensive self-driven course of study and writing. A lifestyle that was to be a very familiar one in Bolinas.

✝

Also, in Bolinas early on was the poet and musician Max Crosley. Crosley and his wife Ruth had drifted into town in the late sixties, following their friend, and Ruth's former husband, Philo T. Farnsworth III, the son of Philo T. Farnsworth II, the inventor of television. Farnsworth, like his father, was a wild genius. He had spent years working on various inventions and experimental music and was busy in Bolinas working over blueprints for a modified kind of geodesic dome (designed to be built from the inside out) which he would later build for himself on the mesa and dub the Yantra House.

Crosley lived on the mesa as well and was developing an early form of performance art, which evolved from the jazz/poetry performances of the Beats. These early performances, which Crosley called "Rituals", involved a group Bolinas jazz musicians who played, as an early collaborator and friend of Crosley, writer Hammond Guthrie wrote, "a unique blend of original composition and jazz standard medleys played around a creatively structured,

11

though to the uneducated ear, chaotic set of improvisations which formed the basic vocabulary of ideas for us to work around." The instruments of this eclectic group included saxes, pianos, trombones, flutes, vibraphones, and an experimental percussion instrument referred to as "The Eternal Machine", which consisted of two picnic tables covered with pocket combs, serving spoons, ten penny nails, castanets, noise-making wind-up toys, and "a variety of woodwind reeds attached to industrial grade garden hoses." Crosley, sometimes along with Guthrie, would create texts to be recited as an integral accompaniment to the music.

‡

Joanne Kyger was born in Vallejo, California in 1934. Her father was a career Navy officer and the family lived for various periods in China, Washington, Florida, Pennsylvania and Illinois. They settled permanently in Santa Barbara, California in 1949 when her father retired. Kyger attended UC Santa Barbara from 1952 to 1956, then moved to San Francisco, where she fell in with the North Beach poetry scene. John Wieners, Robert Duncan, and Jack Spicer were all there at that time. She began to attend the Sunday poetry sessions presided over by Spicer and Duncan, circa 1957 to 1959 in North Beach.

As Kyger remembered, Duncan and Spicer "would read what they had written, and everybody else would read what they had written. And you would be severely criticized. A lot of people would be so heavily criticized that they wouldn't come back."

She also met Lew Welch, Richard Brautigan, Philip Whalen, Ebbe Borregaard, and Gary Snyder during this time. Kyger and Snyder were married in 1960 while they were traveling together in Japan. But the marriage didn't work and after divorcing in 1964 Kyger said, "I just took off on this big energy cruise. I had lots to say to everybody, and it wasn't like playing second fiddle anymore." In 1965 Donald Allen published her first book *The Tapestry and The Web* under his Four Seasons Foundation imprint. The frontispiece of this book was a painting by Jack Boyce.

In a letter dated 1 February 1963, Lew Welch wrote from his hideaway in the Siskiyous to Gary Snyder, "I met a fine fellow, a painter named Jack Boyce. He is intelligent, hip & disgusted with everything and a great lush. Also he can afford to buy good booze. So every week or so I drive 20 miles to his place, or he drives 20 to mine, and we get plastered and talk all night long . . . Jack is one of those artists who spends all his time trying not to be a painter, and who fails nevertheless. He is stuck with it & only needs a small nudge from or into the right direction & he'll blow like crazy. I intend to take him to S.F. in February to see if a tour of our beautiful friends will help."

Lew Welch introduced Boyce to Kyger and the two were married in 1966 and spent 9 months traveling in Europe. When they returned to the U.S., Boyce wanted to try living in New York City for a while because his teacher Richards Rubin from Claremont College in California was living there. The couple found a space to rent on the corner of Grand and Green in the garment district. Boyce partitioned it off with giant timbers and put in a woodburning stove and sleeping loft.

In New York, Kyger and Boyce had a chance to get to know the poets that circulated around the St. Mark's Poetry Project, spending considerable time with Ted Berrigan, Michael Brownstein, Jim Brodey, Anne Waldman and Lewis Warsh, and others. They attended the Waldman/Warsh wedding, which was held at St. Mark's Church. But neither of them were comfortable with the big city life and eventually returned to San Francisco.

In 1969 Joanne Kyger and Jack Boyce were ready to escape to a more rural setting. They moved briefly north of Point Reyes to Bodega Bay, but soon relocated to Bolinas to be near their friends. They bought property on the mesa and lived in a tent while Jack set about building a house.

"It was this immense house," remembers Lewis MacAdams. "He got all these old beams from the Bay Bridge when they had a railroad level, and they tore all that down, and Jack got some of it. God knows how he got it over the hill to Bolinas. Jack was one of these wild guys, the guys that felt they could live outside of the culture and just start it over, even if it meant hauling wood down the coast in a fucking rowboat. Jack was one of those kind of guys."

THE BOLINAS HIT

The beginnings of a real community of writers and artists was taking shape in Bolinas. From various places, and for a variety of reasons, there was a steady influx of newcomers. Notable among these was Ebbe Borregaard, a poet who had been part of the Duncan-Spicer circle in North Beach. Borregaard moved to Bolinas in '69 and initially lived in a tent on Boyce's property. Also on the scene were poets Michael Bond and Lawrence Kearney, along with the graphic artists Arthur Okamura (who had lived in Bolinas since 1960) and Gordon Baldwin (who moved there in July of 1968). Poet Philip Whalen lived at the Doss house for most of the winter of 1968.

Tom Clark, meanwhile, was busy writing letters to poet friends in New York, urging them to visit Bolinas. And they did. Lewis Warsh and Anne Waldman, Larry Fagin, Jim Brodey, Tom Veitch, Ted Berrigan, and Bill Berkson, to name a few, all visited, staying for varying lengths of time in Bolinas between 1968 and 1970.

Another New York refugee in Bolinas at this time was underground comics pioneer and cofounder of the *East Village Other,* Bill Beckman. He and his family were renting space in a building called the Cliffhouse, on the mesa, until they could find more permanent accommodations. Beckman wasted little time before making his presence in Bolinas known via the publication of a crazy little production called *The Bolinas Hit.*

‡

The bastard dream-child of Bill Beckman, *The Bolinas Hit* was a magazine/tabloid publication consisting of eight pages of pure anarchy. The first issue (May 1, 1969) carried a cover photo of two men, pictured from the waist down, dressed in some sort of military or police uniform, complete with jack-boots. One man is kneeing the other in the groin. Inset is the following quote attributed (via Frank O'Hara) to Franz Kline, "To be right is the most terrific personal state that nobody is interested in."

The Hit contained poems, a procedure for the manufacture of LSD, a first-person account of an escape from a Mexican jail, Bill Beckman's "Laying the Foundation" (first in a four part series on the sport of card-house building), and a photo of the bloated tongue of a dead whale ("courtesy of the Hit Culinary Corner").

With a cover price of 25 cents, *The Hit* was printed by the infamous underground comics publisher Rip Off Press in San Francisco. The staff was listed as follows—Publisher: Bill Beckman, Guest Editor: Tom Clark, Hostage Editor: Jim Brodey. In the second (and last) issue, dated June 1, 1969, the staff was listed as Publisher: Bill Beckman, Guest Editor: Tom Clark, Photography: Tom Goodwin, Artists-in-residence: Bill Oetinger and Gordon Baldwin. The cover of the second issue featured a photo of Bolinas resident Bill DesLoge on Brighton Beach wearing a gorilla mask and holding a sign that reads "God is getting pissed". The issue featured a brief excerpt from Bob Dylan's *Tarantula*, poems by Richard Emil Braun, Ron Padgett, John Giorno, David Henderson, Gerard Malanga and Tom Clark, and an article entitled "An Overdose of Hasheesh" reprinted from *Popular Science Monthly*, February, 1884.

The Bolinas Hit was an exercise in social and artistic anarchy, with flourishes of dada-inspired goofiness, as demonstrated in the following bit in the Want Ads:

> Wanted VENUSIAN DOG HAIR. Any
> amount sufficient. Send details
> to Hit, box 242, Bolinas.

It was an inspired and somewhat crazed, totally bohemian, and seriously twisted publication, and in that, a suitable document of Bolinas in 1969.

ON THE MESA

There are so many poets it's hard to see the trees
                    - Tom Clark in a letter to Clark Coolidge, 1970

In the fall of 1969, with his marriage to Anne Waldman essentially over, Lewis Warsh lit out west from New York City. He stayed for a while in Ann Arbor, where Ted Berrigan was teaching, and in Iowa City, then made his way to San Francisco. At the urging of Tom Clark, Warsh settled in at Bolinas, staying initially with the Clarks, then with the Beckmans, and later at the Doss house.

For Lewis Warsh, as for many of the poets who were to live there, Bolinas was a transitional place. Having been so deeply involved in the east side poetry scene in New York, editing the magazine *Angel Hair* and publishing a series of Angel Hair books with Waldman, Warsh often felt out of synch in California. He was never sure that he wanted to stay in Bolinas but didn't really know where else he could go. He spent most of his time with Tom Clark. The two wrote several collaborations, notably a set of poems that was published under the title *Chicago* – which was the first Angel Hair Book out of Bolinas and was printed by Andrew Hoyem in San Francisco in 1969.

During this time Warsh was writing letters, sometimes daily, to Bill Berkson in New York. These letters form an interesting real time commentary on life in Bolinas:

> Everyone here works very hard during the day, building houses, that seems like the big male trip everyone's on, though the consciousness behind it can't be put down, it

just isn't mine. Left with long hours to fill pleasurably with Tom, Joanne & myself (Jack, J's husband, is one of the house-builders mentioned above) [. . .] Life at Tom's very quiet. Play with the baby, eat homemade Angelica cookies, radio, TV, records, lots of dope. The Bolinas social scene as I see it consists of lots of people who for various reasons wish to be here in Bolinas at this moment in time & that's what brings them together, that's their base. What they do in real life is another thing altogether. I haven't gone into it very deeply but both Tom & Joanne are involved with "it"—have to live with it—to various degrees. A very weird sort of community & definitely a scene, though traveling has made me realize that there are millions of different scenes going on all over every minute with dope & music & one hopes poetry moving in circles around the center which is everyone's inter relations.

(Letter to Bill Berkson
November 3 Monday [1969])

Much of Warsh's book *Part of My History* (Coach House Press 1971) deals with his time in Bolinas. Once piece in this book entitled "California Diary,1969", describes a typical day of wandering about the mesa, dropping acid, meeting people, listening to music, writing poetry, drinking wine and smoking grass.

Joanne Kyger had separated from Jack Boyce during the winter of 1969-1970. Warsh and Kyger had a brief romance shortly thereafter. In his book *Long Distance* (Ferry Press, 1971), Lewis Warsh asks the particularly Bolinasian question, "Can poets live together?":

. . . To break down the walls
which separate each other's houses. To open the doors
of the rooms in which we sit, privately, contemplating
our works, each other's works, the works of the gods of
the past, present & future, to exist as if there were
only one room & fill it with all the poets you like

Warsh sees it as "just another typical domestic scene" only with a difference that lends a "fragility to our acts, as if we were participants in a / softer sense of ourselves."

> . . . If I resemble
> you, well, that's an accident - I didn't mean to be mistaken
> for anyone, not even myself.

‡

Bill Berkson first visited Bolinas briefly during Christmas and New Year, 1969-70. Gordon Baldwin was out of town at the time, and Tom Clark and Lewis Warsh had arranged for Berkson to stay at Baldwin's apartment. Also visiting over the holidays was Ted Berrigan and Alice Notley. There was a group reading on the mesa at Mary Coleman's house—a house where, as local legend has it, Isadora Duncan had danced. The reading included Berkson, Berrigan, Ebbe Borregaard, Tom Clark, Joanne Kyger, John Thorpe, and Lewis Warsh.

Berkson remembered being greatly impressed, "bowled over, really", by the coastal landscape and the "dramatic scale human relations seemed to take on within it". He returned to New York, but by the early spring of 1970 had decided to pack up and move to California.

In June of 1970 Berkson rented a car and drove cross-country with Jim Carroll and Devereaux Carson (Carroll's then girlfriend). On the way they stopped at Allen Ginsberg's farm in Cherry Valley, and then at Niagara Falls. In Mount Gilead, Ohio, they picked up their friend Jayne Nodland who accompanied them on the rest of the trip. The rental car died at Arroyo Hondo, New Mexico, where they visited poet Harris Schiff who was living in a commune there. They got a replacement rental car in Santa Fe and drove headlong to California. Carroll was sick with heroin withdrawal and complained constantly so they drove nonstop from New Mexico to San Francisco, where they stayed for a night in a Portrero Hill house shared by the Lewis and Phoebe MacAdams and Bill and Nancy Presson. The next day Berkson, Carroll and Carson drove up to Bolinas. The junk-sick version of the cross-country trip

18

can be found in Carroll's poem "Withdrawal Letter" in his book *Living at the Movies* (Grossman, 1973).

Berkson began to make arrangements to stay indefinitely in Bolinas, while Carroll, still sick, was all too eager to hop a plane and get back to New York. Carroll wasn't impressed by Bolinas, as Berkson recalled he said it was "too white". His "California Poem", also printed in *Living at the Movies*, would seem to summarize his impression of Bolinas. It ends with the following lines:

and out here poets sleep beaches all day
with fears of Japan where bronze children
start landslides on their brains

The week that Berkson relocated he was surprised to find out that he was to take part in a reading of "Nine Bolinas Poets" organized by Andrew Hoyem at the San Francisco Museum of Art. The nine poets included Joanne Kyger, John Thorpe, Tom Clark, Lewis Warsh, Ebbe Borregaard, Lawrence Kearney, and Michael Bond.

Berkson initially stayed with Warsh in the house near Agate Beach. There was some jealousy and uneasiness on Kyger's part regarding Berkson's arrival, but once that was resolved (in what Berkson described as a "memorable meeting" in a driveway in town), the two became close friends and soon rented the Waring House on Brighton Road in downtown Bolinas.

Warsh left Bolinas in September for a brief trip to New York. He returned to California in the spring of 1971, staying in San Francisco until the summer when he moved to Stinson Beach, sharing a house with underground cartoonist Greg Irons and his wife Evan, just down the street from where poet Tom Veitch and his wife Martha were living.

Berkson and Kyger eventually shared the Waring house, later to be known as the Grand Hotel, with Peter Warshall (who initially came to Bolinas to visit the Creeleys who lived down the street) and Keith Lampe (a former Yippie, who went by the name Ponderosa Pine). The house became a kind of social center, a place where primarily poets would drop by, and hang out, and where many parties and readings took place. When the property was sold in 1971,

Kyger and Berkson each bought a house on the mesa, within a block of each other.

‡

After dealing with the draft board in Texas, Lewis MacAdams and his wife Phoebe eventually made their way to San Francisco in 1968. Although they had visited several times, the couple didn't have any interest in moving to Bolinas at the time. "It just seemed too far in the country," MacAdams said. They moved back to New York and didn't return to California until 1970. This time their destination was Bolinas.

They moved into "this incredible, funky house", just down the road from Tom Clark's house on the mesa overlooking Duxbury Reef and the vast Pacific. "I had never lived outside a city in my life," MacAdams said, "and it was like, oh, God, I was hypnotized. We were having a baby, and having this disastrous emotional life, and all I really wanted to do was just sit and stare out the window—which I did a lot, actually."

‡

In late 1970, poet Robert Creeley, who had just landed a visiting professor's position at San Francisco State University, moved his wife, the writer Bobbie Louise Hawkins, and their daughters, out to Bolinas. He chose Bolinas because of the friends that were living there—Arthur Okamura and Joanne Kyger, in particular. The Creeley's lived at first in the Dowd House on Brighton Ave, then moved to a big New England style house on Terrace Avenue. Creeley was widely respected by a number of the poets in Bolinas and his arrival was eagerly anticipated.

Poet John Clarke, who had spent time in Bolinas during the summer of 1968 and again during the summer of 1970, wrote an intriguing book that dealt with Bolinas and the impending arrival of Robert Creeley. The poets of Bolinas were the principals in this book, a Blakean masque, that Clarke wrote as part of the Curriculum of the Soul series. In 1968 Charles Olson composed "A Plan for a Curriculum of the Soul" which was subsequently published in *The Magazine of Further Studies*. After Olson's death in 1970, Clarke assigned topics from Olson's plan to selected poets and these were published as fascicles in the Curriculum of the Soul series. Clarke's own assignment was:

> "Poets as such, that is disciplined lives not
>   history or for any 'art' reasons example
> Blake
>   the same, say, medicine man"

Taking Blake's life as "order", arranged in 21 movements, including "textual and speech event as well as chronological sequence of his life," Clarke let the poets of Bolinas act it out, as he said, "so that if they had not 'disciplined lives' in the Blake sense Olson means it individually, they could have it all together, that is, collectively, each satisfying some aspect of the whole 'form', and speaking the Blake quotes appropriate to that progressive movement (interspersed with contemporary talk), which I then thought could perhaps activate both ways, both Blake and Bolinas, through play, life to the level of 'medicine'."

Crucial then to the plot of this play was the anticipation of Creeley's arrival in town. The climax of which was the transformation of Creeley as Ulro into Eden—Blake's lowest to highest condition—corresponding to a moment in Blake's prophetic poem, *Jerusalem*.

Published in 1973, John Clarke's *Blake: A Mask* (dedicated to Jack Boyce) is a wildly visionary take on the poets of Bolinas, often very funny, especially as the lofty Blakean prophetic language bumps up against the colloquial, but also insightful in its careful portrayal of the relationships between the poets there.

‡

Darrel DeVore was a musician, composer and experimental instrument maker. He was playing jazz piano in Missouri before moving to San Francisco in the sixties and helping to form the psychedelic band The Charlatans, who recorded for Mercury Records but dissolved soon after. DeVore meanwhile was offered a contract with a pop recording label but walked out in the middle of negotiations. He'd had enough of the commercial music scene and began to focus upon his own compositions and the making of strange new experimental musical instruments, such as the wind-wand, the bamboo xylophone, and the circular violin. He married Robert Creeley's daughter Kirsten, in a ceremony conducted by Lewis MacAdams. "He was a huge influence on my way of seeing and hearing and doing," MacAdams said of DeVore, "He was an inspired soul. I learned a lot from him."

DeVore promoted a kind of radical free music which he called Universal Music. He described it as "The fusing of primitive Aboriginal spirit with modern technology and synthesis derived from all the world music cultures, results in 'Universal Music'." It was in this spirit that DeVore and Tom Veitch came up with the idea of the Poet's Orchestra. The announcement for their first performance is vintage Bolinas:

ATTENTION, FOLKS
A most unusual occasion figures to be this coming Sunday,
JANUARY 17 at the clock of 8:30 PM or thereabouts
behind the restful doors of THE BOLINAS COMMUNITY
CENTER when strange blast of sunshine and moon music
be erupting for a couple of hours or so, strange love gut
notes of POEM and NOISE upon unusual and rare flame
performance of
THE BOLINAS POETS ORCHESTRA
! ! !
To enter the magic dimension will cost a smear of coin, 35¢
or 50¢ at the door to be exact. A few will be allowed to join
the backhanded craziness if they can by waving a little
yellow flag and running up on the stage and doing three
eskimo handstands. Many FAMOUS POETS and MUSIC
DOCTORS will pe4m together for the first time in 2,000
years of Western Sadness. I sat smoking a cigarette and
watching out of the upper window as the cops chased a
nude girl through the park. Later I went to the doctor and
was alarmed to find out that my blood pressure was very
low. I hope this won't spoil my summer trip to pan for gold
. . .
SPECIAL GUEST STARS: THE YELLOW MANDARIN
and

THE GHOST OF ALBERT AYLER!
plus John Lennon, The Rolling Stones, and many more . . .

The Poets Orchestra, which only performed a couple of times, was a loose amalgam of musicians and poets, including Berkson, Kyger, MacAdams, and Tom Clark, all of whom played or toyed with various instruments ranging from guitars and saxes to assorted percussion ding-dongs and pieces of kelp. While similar in spirit to Max Crosley's "Rituals", The Poets Orchestra was an exercise in free music with virtually no underlying structure at all. Tom Clark described the first performance in a letter to Clark Coolidge as "Periods of unison dotting huge seas of cacophony." "The idea," Clark said later, "was to build up this din wherein the individual faults and graces of the instrumentalists would never be noticed."

The Poets Orchestra performed at the Bolinas Community Center and at the Hansen Fuller Gallery in San Francisco.

‡

One of the members of The Poets Orchestra was the poet and musician David Meltzer. Meltzer was an accomplished guitarist, having played with the group Serpent Power in the sixties. He had close ties to Wallace Berman and his influential Beat underground magazine Semina and was a force on the San Francisco poetry scene. Meltzer, his wife Tina and their three daughters moved to Bolinas in 1969. Tina worked as a teacher at the Bolinas school. Joanne Kyger remembered the warm, hospitable scene at the Meltzer home—"There were singing parties. David would play guitar and Tina would sing. She had a beautiful voice."

‡

Joel Weishaus, a poet who first visited Bolinas in early 1969, then later that year stayed at the Doss house on Brighton, decided in 1970 that the literary scene in Bolinas was so rich it deserved an anthology. He went door to door, poet to poet, asking for manuscripts and soon had the makings for a modest anthology. Since he was at that time working for an outfit in San Francisco called The Company & Sons, an underground comics publisher that was looking to branch out into publishing books, he first thought that they could publish the anthology. Unfortunately, the owners of The Company & Sons were, as Weishaus put it, "so freaky and paranoid", that he became worried about the "safety" of the manuscript. He quit the company taking the manuscript with him and offered it to Lawrence Ferlinghetti and City Lights. Ferlinghetti wasn't very enthusiastic about the project, but Weishaus was persistent, and Ferlinghetti finally agreed to print the book.

On the Mesa: An Anthology of Bolinas Writing was published in 1971 by City Lights. The book included work by Michael Bond, David Meltzer, Max Crosley, Robert Creeley, Ebbe Borregaard, Joanne Kyger, Tom Clark, Bill Berkson, John Doss, Keith Lampe, Bill Brown, John Thorpe, Lawrence Kearney, and Lewis Warsh, with a frontispiece drawn by Arthur Okamura and including a drawing by Gordon Baldwin. A note on the back of the book reads:

> This is a gathering of poets and writers and artists living in or around the mesa in Bolinas, California. Not so much a school of poets as a meeting of those who happen to be at this geographical location at this point in wobbly time, several divergent movements in American poetry of the past 20 years (Black Mountain, San Francisco Beat, "New York School" of poets) have come together with new Western and mystic elements at the unpaved crossroads of Bolinas.

While there were several magazines and journals that were devoted to Bolinas writing, *On the Mesa* was the first, and only, anthology of Bolinas writers.

Also printed on the back cover is this quote from poet Daniel Moore (who had lived in Bolinas for a brief time in the late sixties):

> Like those Rabelaisian characters who took to the mountaintops during the plague and caroused and told stories completely unharmed by the plague while the plague went on below them, like those in Noah's boat who took to high ground during the flood, like those who "hold back the

edges of [their] gowns . . . for we are going through Hell," so these poets have taken to the Bolinas Mesa, high ground, while the world goes awash around them, practicing a little "Black Mountainery," a little "New York Schoolery," and a little Tom Foolery. All part of America's vital poetic machinery, high on the Mesa.

Moore is somewhat over romantic here, but that sense of Bolinas as refuge was very real.

"The first few years I lived in Bolinas I did not want to go into the City," MacAdams said, "I really wanted to root myself in Bolinas . . . I didn't even like to look at San Francisco across the water!" This sentiment was shared not only by the poets but most people living in Bolinas. A sentiment that was soon to become a cause in itself.

SITTING IN THE CONTROL ROOM OF THE WIZARD OF OZ

A t 1:45 am on the morning of Monday, January 18, 1971, the tanker Oregon Standard was rammed by its sister ship, the Arizona Standard, in dense fog just outside the Golden Gate. Two of its tanks ruptured spilling between 500,000 and 1.9 million gallons of bunker oil into the Pacific.

On the morning of Tuesday, January 19, the oil washed up on the shore of Bolinas.

"We just got up one morning ," Tom Clark remembered, "and everything smelled like oil." Clark knocked on Lewis MacAdams' door at 9:00 a.m. to give him the bad news.

Sculptor Tom D'Onofrio first heard news of the spill early that morning on the radio. He ran out of his house, jumped on his horse, and headed for the beach. "I could smell the oil before I got to the cliff [at Agate Beach]. I got there and looked down and the beach was covered with oil. It was on the rocks, the waves, the logs. Everything. And I started to cry. I'll never forget that moment."

D'Onofrio's first thought was of Bolinas Lagoon, a haven for migratory birds and seals, and home to a wide variety of native birds and fishes. Thankfully the oil had yet to enter the lagoon, but D'Onofrio knew something had to be done before the next high tide. He called upon his neighbor John Armstrong, and they came up with a plan to construct a boom, made of logs, which would be strung together at the narrow entrance to the lagoon. "It was a crude plan," D'Onofrio said, "but this was instantaneous thinking." He then headed down to Wharf Road to round up volunteers.

By the time MacAdams made it down to the beach dozens of people were gathering. The next high tide was at noon, there wasn't enough time to build the wooden boom and get it into place, so bales of hay were being dropped off for the construction of a temporary boom. "Everything we do is a guess," MacAdams wrote in his account of the spill, *A Bolinas Report* (Zone Press, 1971). A Standard Oil crew was on the scene constructing another barricade across the lagoon, this one a 3-foot-high piece of plastic, which almost immediately was broken by the rush of the flood tide and sank.

Literally hundreds of volunteers showed up, spreading hay at the mouth of the lagoon and along the beach. MacAdams hooked up with Peter Warshall, who has been supervising the bird recovery efforts at the Marine Biology Center, and together they walked up the beach giving advice to groups of people working to save the birds that were washing up on the sand covered in oil.

The next day Macadams reports that some of the Standard Oil crew, along with Jack Boyce, Michael Bond, and a few other Bolinas citizens, were huddled around John Armstrong who was drawing a diagram in the wet sand of the boom he was proposing to build across the mouth of the lagoon. Logs and wood were hastily brought down to the beach and work on the boom began.

The boom was put together quickly and it worked to keep most of the oil out of the lagoon, but it didn't hold against the high tide that rolled in at midnight. MacAdams joined the crew pulling oil-soaked hay from the lagoon. They worked till dawn and were covered in the thick, sticky bunker oil. Getting the oil off your body was a difficult procedure. As MacAdams explained it, "First you wash in diesel fuel. Then you dry off with rags. Then you wash with cold cream. Then you dry off with rags. Then you wash with soap and water and dry off and you're ready for a dry cheeseburger."

A larger boom was built by Armstrong, Bond, Boyce and company. This boom held while three other barriers that were later built by Standard Oil to reinforce the barricade gave way.

During all of these efforts there were mounting tensions between the Standard Oil crew and the Bolinas volunteers. Standard Oil threatened to call in the state police to keep the Bolinas people off the beach. But there was little faith among the locals that Standard Oil knew what they were doing. It was up to them, the people of Bolinas, to take charge and respond to the crisis.

Greg Hewlett, described by MacAdams as "a real crazy, visionary guy", who had worked with Tom Hayden in Newark, was one of the prime movers in the initial response and subsequent political mobilization of Bolinas, as was Peter Warshall, who was in the process of becoming professional naturalist and environmental advocate/activist. He was about to receive a PHD in Primate Studies from Harvard.

Hewlett said of the town's response to the crisis, "It was an incredible combination of individuals and a goal, and a real caring for what was going on in a place that we really love. There's no way you can recapture the energy that was going on at the time. In those first few days, we pulled some shit off that was borderline miraculous."

Russ Riviere recalls setting up a communications station in the marine biology laboratory—"There were three of us on seven phones probably 24 hours a day for a week. We simply decided what we needed, called to get it, and told them to send the bill to Standard Oil. We really didn't know what we were doing, but we pretended pretty well. It was like sitting in the control room of the Wizard of Oz."

Bolinas became headline news. TV crews rolled into town along with marine biologists, squads of workers from Standard Oil, and volunteers by the truckload. Still others showed up with food for the volunteers. Bolinas was soon inundated with thousands of people. The narrow streets were filled with trucks, tractors, bulldozers, and back-hoes. Helicopters were continually circling overhead. By all accounts it was an incredible scene.

Unfortunately, the effort to save the birds who were coated in the thick bunker oil was largely futile. "We saved maybe five out of every 100 birds," Hewlett said. "We tried everything, from corn meal to olive oil to detergent. A lot of it didn't work. This wasn't oil, this was tar."

It is estimated that the spill killed upwards of 20,000 birds.

‡

One year later Peter Warshall wrote, "We got luck. There's no doubt. Each time another report spells out the consequences of the oil spill, I hear the song: Bolinas must be blessed". Warshall goes on to explain that the Oregon and Arizona Standard tankers were loaded with Bunker C petroleum which flows easily only at temperatures around 122 degrees Fahrenheit. In the cool Pacific waters, it forms an asphalt like goo that floats. Another blessing was the weather, there were no storms—had there been, the slick would have most likely covered the entire lagoon and the results could have been much worse.

The most profound and lasting effect of the spill was in how it changed Bolinas. The energy generated by the community's response to the crisis carried over into local politics. Hewlett, Riviere, Warshall, MacAdams, and others got together and formed the Bolinas Future Studies Center, dedicated to the development of alternative forms of energy, agriculture, waste disposal, and housing. The mission was to keep Bolinas from becoming a coastal version of Mill Valley—a threat that was very real at the time.

The group went door-to-door, organized neighborhood meetings, and soon delivered some major impacts. They initiated a recall of the directors of the Bolinas Community Public Utility District, which was the closest thing to a government entity in this unincorporated municipality. They then set about drafting a community plan and blocked all future development by imposing a strict moratorium on new water hook-ups.

Their first major victory was stopping the Kennedy Sewer project, an ambitious plan to link Stinson Beach and Bolinas through one sewer system. Under the plan, not only would sewage have been released in the ocean, but the larger capacity sewage system would have invited development, perhaps adding tens of thousands of people to the population. There was intense pressure from the county to enact the Kennedy Plan. The antiquated sewage system in Bolinas, which only extended from the downtown area to the little mesa, was dumping into Bolinas lagoon. After halting the Kennedy Plan, the BPUD was charged with proposing a viable sewage alternative for the town. After much research and debate on the subject, a progressive solution was found in the creation of sewer ponds, a system that worked along lines similar to those of a septic tank.

This heightened political awareness and action in the community was a direct result of the oil spill. The people of Bolinas realized how tenuous the parameters of their community really were and that it was up to them to preserve and protect their town.

A DIARY OF COMMUNITY CONSCIOUSNESS

O n July 6, 1971 a new publication hit the streets of Bolinas. The oblong newsletter featured this note on its cover:

> DEAR READERS,
> Welcome to the first issue of THE PAPER.
> We hope you enjoy it and we also hope
> that THE PAPER fairly represents our
> town. We want THE PAPER to be a true
> community paper, not the ravings of a
> minority element. In this paper every-
> body can rave. Each issue will be open
> and flexible. The size, appearance,
> and content will evolve with the needs
> of our town. Hopefully our town will
> be a place without fear, where under-
> standing and sympathy are as strong as
> the wind.

Edited and published by Bill Beckman, the first issue of *The Paper* sold for ten cents and carried a report on the School Board Meeting, an article on water conservation, gardening tips and a report from the Future Studies Center. The name "Bolinas" is never used in this first issue. In some places it is simply blanked out, other times only the initial B. is used. On the back was a photograph by Ilka Hartmann of an oil covered fist raised in defiance. The caption read "lest we forget January 1971". *The Paper* also carried this prohibition, "NOT TO BE SOLD EAST OF MT. TAMALPAIS".

The Paper was a significant change from Beckman's earlier bit of loony anarchy, *The Bolinas Hit*. It was a result of the oil spill and the rallying of the townspeople, who for the first time began to think of themselves as a community. While Bolinas had its share of zonked-out hippies, there was among them not only a contingent of serious poets, but a very well-educated group of young people, several of whom were former 1960s campus radicals. After the wake-up call that came in the form of the oil spill, it became clear that the only way for the town to survive was to come together, on a grass-roots level, and take over the destiny of Bolinas.

The strict growth limits and progressive land-use plans proposed by the Future Studies Center and executed by the BPUD were designed to keep the community small and manageable, on an ecological level. On another level, it was seen as a symptom of an isolationist paranoia (one that could be symbolized by the theft of the Bolinas road-sign, the first incident of which occurred around this time). To many this isolationism was a way of protecting Bolinas. It was taboo to mention the name "Bolinas" to anyone "outside". There were even plans proposed in *The Paper* to make Wharf Road and Brighton Ave one-way streets, pointing out of town.

Issues #7 and #8 of *The Paper* featured, in two installments, a Greg Irons cartoon entitled "The Creature From The Bolinas Lagoon". The cartoon, which originally appeared in the first issue of Berkson's magazine *Big Sky*, was an ecological horror story of what would happen to Bolinas if the proposed county sewer plan was put into effect.

Reading the early issues of *The Paper*, one can clearly track the new direction of Bolinas and the work in building a community. This community building was later documented by Orville Schell in his 1974 book *The Town That Fought to Save Itself*. Schell, a Bolinas resident, presented a social study of the Whole Earth Catalog mind-set of organic farming and community building that was at the core of life in Bolinas at that time. Illustrated with photographs by Ilka Hartmann, Schell's book provides an inside look at the central principles and concerns of the Bolinas community during this period.

Interesting to note that Schell, careful to observe the taboo of mentioning the name "Bolinas" to outsiders, changes the name of the town to "Briones"—the name of one of the early founding families of Bolinas.

‡

The Paper, which in 1973 was renamed *Beaulines: A Diary of Community Consciousness*, was the voice of the community. The ongoing reports of School Board and BPUD meetings kept the town aware of local politics, while various articles on composting, organic gardening, and local gossip all provide a window onto the general consciousness and concerns of the town. In issue #12 (April 8, 1972), there is a short piece entitled "Friday Night" which was "gathered from contemporary reports" by Lewis MacAdams. The article is an account of Greg Hewlitt getting "fantastically drunk" and generally raising havoc, which ultimately resulted in Greg breaking his shoulder and collarbone trying to make a getaway on a stolen bicycle. MacAdams, writing under the pseudonym Dorko Solingen, later had a regular gossip column called "Constant Comment" that appeared in *Beaulines*.

Poems also made the pages of *The Paper* and *Beaulines*. This was a community that valued and respected their poets, just as the poets, for the most part, valued and respected the community. Creeley, for example, wrote poems for the graduating class at the Bolinas School in '71, '72, and '73. However, *The Paper* and *Beaulines* included not only poems from the many known poets who were living there, but poems by anyone who sent them in. This democratic editorship, printing just about anything what was given you, was to be employed later in a couple of other Bolinas publications and is indicative of the philosophic bent of the community. The May 12, 1972, issue of *The Paper* included a small untitled poem by Ellen Sander:

> I swear to God
> Me and Angelica
> w/Juliet
> met a diabetic monkey
> in a tree on Hawthorne
> in the Sheriff's yard

and if that is not as good
as Tom or Bob or Lewis or Joanne or even Bill can do
You Can Kiss My Ass

As Lewis MacAdams said, "It's all sort of obvious, but what the outside world thought of as the Bolinas poets was not quite who the Bolinas people thought of as the Bolinas poets. It included those poets, because everybody knew who they were and respected them, more or less, because there were a lot of literate people there, and there were some great poets, but a lot of people just weren't impressed by that."

A long time Bolinas fixture is the Free Box on Wharf Road. The Free Box was a wooden box into which townspeople could place unwanted items, primarily clothing, that could in turn be taken by anyone who had use for them. Rescued from the Free Box, and finding its way into the hands of Joanne Kyger, was a journal kept by local boat-builder John Armstrong. An entry in that journal may well reflect the perception some Bolinas residents had about the proliferation of New York poets in the town circa 1970:

All the half-assed poets holding hands
New York City creep literary! scene.

Armstrong then immediately offers what he believes to be the Bolinas alternative, writing directly beneath the entry quoted above, "John Thorpe—good for John Thorpe, so strong."

‡

In 1971 Bobbie Louise Hawkins wrote a Bolinas column for *The Point Reyes Light*, a weekly newspaper published in nearby Point Reyes Station. The column, "The Bolinas Other", was a sampling of Bolinas social and cultural news, most of which featured the resident poets. The Thursday, October 14, 1971 column starts with the tale of "Joanne Kyger's New Roof" and goes on to a list of "Great Books Lately Published by Locals"— *Scenes of Life at the Capital* by Philip Whalen, *Desecheo Notebook* by Joanne Kyger, *165 Meeting House Lane* by Alice Notley, and *Two Serious Poems and One Other* by Bill Berkson and Larry Fagin. Hawkins makes mention of recent visitors (Robert Duncan, Gary Snyder, Richard Brautigan) and of Guggenheim grants awarded to Robert Creeley and Tom Clark. She lists some friends who are traveling (Whalen to New York, Lynn O'Hare to Oaxaca, Kearney to Disneyland, Berkson to "the Big Apple"), and ends with a note about Donald Allen's new Grey Fox Press.

‡

Ted Berrigan and Alice Notley lived in Bolinas during the summer and fall of 1971. As Notley remembered, "Ted was pleased to be near Bob Creeley, Joanne Kyger, Bill Berkson, Tom Clark, etc., but he found the organic vegetable and milk your own goat scene extremely delirious-making."

Notley and Berrigan stayed with Lewis MacAdams during their visit. As MacAdams remembered, "There was never anybody less real in Bolinas than Ted. Except at night. He and Alice were doing a lot of speed and so they never wanted to be out in the daylight. They'd stay in and read and come out at night. Alice never went out; Ted went down to the bar."

MacAdams also felt that Berrigan had no patience for MacAdams' interest and involvement in local politics. "It just didn't seem worthwhile to him," said MacAdams.

Berrigan and Tom Clark wrote a book-length collaboration entitled *Bolinas Eyewash*. A very brief excerpt from *Bolinas Eyewash* appeared in *The Paper*, (#7, Nov. 15, 1971), and an excerpt titled "8 Snippets from Bolinas Eyewash" was printed in 1972 in a little magazine out of Chicago called *Oink*.

The manuscript of *Bolinas Eyewash* is 103 pages of very free association, or disassociation, all swirling about the Bolinas scene of 1971. Nothing, and no one, is sacred:

> Last Friday night the Attorney General of the State of
> California filed suit against the people of Bolinas to wit that
> the people of Bolinas cease to dispose of their sewage in
> their customary matter at once, or pay a fine of $6,000 a
> day until they do so. Mr. Shao Thorpe of Hawthorne Road
> replied, "I don't have any money but I'll be glad to give the
> Attorney General some of this here broccoli."

- - - - - - - - -

The word of mouth network plugs you in to what's happening inside everybody else's houses, even if you never go there, & don't even want to.

- - - - - - - - -

BOLINAS
get, in the complexity of our present
responsible elements seething between
impasto excitation & somber, subtly evoked granduer.

- - - - - - - - -

I run into the popular novelist; he's seated on a fireplug at the corner of Barf Road & Wrighton Ave. I ask "what's happening?" & he reply, "Well I'm just waiting for Lewis MacAdams who's gonna meet me here, wearing a hamburger."

- - - - - - - - -

The professionals are convinced that Bolinas would be an ideal precedent setter for the proper management of human waste.

- - - - - - - - -

Tommy Nobis & MacArthur Lane come over for dinner with Bob Creeley, John the Butcher, Lucy Rose & young Gus. A good time is had by all except or maybe especially Bob, who keeps wrapping Scotch Tape around his head & yelling things like "Iwo Jima" and "Not Absurdly!"

- - - - - - - - -

We swear not to give in to the outside forces that want to twist our words and our tongues and ignore our wishes and dreams of a wide berth on the planet in harmony with our brothers and sisters by pressuring us into a surf ghetto bordering on further subdivisions of the meatball, right?

- - - - - - - - -

It is God's wish that no waste be discharged into any water. We must maintain integrity with the mountains & the sea. Waste is waste, that's all there is to it.

- - - - - - - - -

Every day another Chlorine Rap.

Berrigan's clock wasn't right for Bolinas. He was a big city guy and the pastoral setting of Bolinas just didn't work for him. In his poem "Things To Do In Bolinas", Berrigan lists such interesting activities as "watch the natives suffer—freeze & sleep—yearn for city lights." In a piece entitled "From Journals: BOLINAS", published in *The World* in 1973, Berrigan offers this summation:

> Bolinas, in the final analysis, for you, for me, there is,
> alas, quote unquote No Use.
> > The black eye is your favorite salutation.
> I don't have time to suffer.

LOTS OF DOGS / LOTS OF DOPE

B errigan's longtime friend, the artist Joe Brainard, also visited Bolinas in 1971. *Bolinas Journal*, (Big Sky Books, 1971), Brainard's account of his visit, offers a brilliant, perceptive, often very funny, portrait of the place:

> Bolinas is more like I thought Jamaica would be than Jamaica was. (So lush). And fantastic flowers everywhere. A lot of talk about things I don't know much about. Like eastern religions. Ecology. And local problems. Sewer problems in particular.
>
> - - - - - - - - -
>
> A lot of being inside your own head here. A lot of talk about it. And a lot of talk about being inside other people's heads too.
>
> - - - - - - - - -
>
> Bolinas dogs are so funny. Running around all over town. In and out of stores. Alone or in packs. Plain dogs most of them. Mutts. They seem to have a little Bolinas all their own. With rules and regulations I'm sure I couldn't begin to fathom.
>
> - - - - - - - - -
>
> Lots of dogs.
> Lots of dope.
>
> - - - - - - - - -
>
> Bolinas is such a basic place. The land being so important. Survival seems to be the main issue.
>
> - - - - - - - - -
>
> The impossibility of living here strikes again. (Night)

Brainard notes, "Living in Bolinas is turning out to be very like living in New York City."

Bolinas certainly had more than its share of transplanted New Yorkers. As Philip Whalen noted in his book-length poem *Scenes of Life at the Capital* (Grey Fox Press, 1971), "Who is there to see in New York anyway / Everybody's moved to Bolinas."

‡

During part of his stay in Bolinas, Brainard shared a house with Philip Whalen, who had recently returned from a year in Japan. Whalen had written to Margot Doss from Japan, hoping to stay at the Doss house in Bolinas upon his return. The Doss house was spoken for at that time, but Margot found a room for him at the Webber house which was near the Creeley's home on Terrace Avenue. Later in 1971, Donald Allen, the editor of the landmark anthology *The New American Poetry*, bought a house on Kale Road on the mesa, and Whalen rented the "guest wing" there until the middle of February 1972.

In an early Bolinas poem, "America inside & outside Bill Brown's House in Bolinas" (from *Severance Pay*, 1970), Whalen deftly interweaves a description of the landscape of the mesa with a prevalent Bolinas attitude in a few lines:

> Flowers thick and various, fuchsias all over everything
> Houses all scattered, all different, unrelated to the ground
> or to each other except by road and waterpipe
> Each person isolated, carefully watching for some guy
> to make some funny move & then let him have it POW
> Right on the beezer

In the same book, this little vignette, from a poem titled "Life at Bolinas. The Last of California. For Margot & John Doss":

> At Duxbury Point, a few thousand feet from here
> The wind blows heavy 35 miles an hour all night long
> Big lights at the post office illuminate Brighton Avenue
> The raccoons can see to get across

The Bolinas dogs were a problem. Packs of dogs roamed the downtown area, the beach and the mesa. Whalen said the dogs were "pests". In his poem "The Turn" (in *The Kindness of Strangers*, 1976) he describes an encounter with some Bolinas dogs:

> Walking along Elm Road
> Handful of nasturtiums, butter, some kind of bread
> 75¢ the loaf no advertising included
> Bread and air and a price tag wrapped in plastic
> The dogs come out as usual to roar at me
> I find myself screeching wildly in reply
> Fed up with suppressing my rage and fear
> I bellow and roar
> The dogs are scared and their people scandalized
> "What are you trying to do? HAY! What are you trying to do?"
> I had nothing to tell them, I was talking to their dogs.

Like Berrigan and Clark, Whalen shows some impatience with living in Bolinas:

> All these people out here (i.e. Bolinas)
> All of them shouting
> (They are "in the country")
> A head full of discontented screams,
> Roars, motor noises, rockets,
> Extraterrestrial ray guns, dogs,
> Chickens, carpenters, noon whistle (all the way from
> Stinson Beach,
> population 84, an air-raid siren, just imagine!)
> The blue sky clabbering up to rain?
> (from "Weather Odes" in *The Kindness of Strangers*, 1976)

Whalen said that his reasons for leaving Bolinas in 1972 were "too many parties, too many tourists and the difficulty of getting to and from the City". In "A Letter, to Bill Berkson" (in *The Kindness of Strangers*) Whalen gives this farewell to Bolinas:

There are no poems today.
Bolinas: too many people
            not enough
            W A T E R
No solitude where too many
cars, telephones, dogs—
No see no hear nothing.
Too bad! I go away.
All the trails overgrown with bushes
            vines and kookaburrs.
            Dead beaches. Ripped-out heads.
            G O O D B Y E.

TILTH

C oming to Bolinas and getting involved in politics saved my life," Lewis MacAdams said, "I understood that that was what you could do, you could make it, you could start from the ground up, you know, make sure the water was right."

MacAdams became deeply involved in town politics and working with the Future Studies Center, helping to outline the new radical principles of Bolinas. He was the scribe for the Bolinas Community Plan in 1974, as well as the Bolinas section of the Marin County General Plan.

MacAdams also wrote *A Bolinas Report*, an on-the-spot piece of early gonzo journalism describing the effects of the oil spill on the town, which was first published in an underground newspaper in New York, then by Zone Press (with a brilliant cover drawing by Greg Irons). In 1972 he published a book of interviews with Bolinas townspeople about their gardens and the progressive organic farming methods that were being employed. The book, *Tilth*, included photographs by Phoebe MacAdams, and was printed by the Mesa Press and published by the Bolinas Future Studies Center. The word "tilth" comes from the Middle English "tilian", meaning "to till". It is defined as cultivated land, or "the aggregation of soil in relation to its suitability for crop growth." Organic farming and progressive land and water management, along with prohibitions on population growth and building, were the essentials of Bolinas politics. Naturally this engagement with local politics made its way into some of MacAdams' poems:

> DIRECTORS OF THE P.U.D.
> Last night we sat around the table plotting how to
> spend the town's money wisely. Orville said...

something. Bill, his sleepy eyes,
he ate granola. Does Paul know himself?
Flushed, his fingers move across an envelope.
Orville, pale, holds his heart. His forehead throbs
and Paul discerns a new bottom line.
Bill pops wood into the fire and spins around.
We must face our neighbors with this information.
Is it right?
(from *Live at the Church*, by Lewis MacAdams,
Kulchur, 1977)

MacAdams' poetry of the time reveals an engagement with not only local politics but with his family and friends, as well as the people and the place itself. "Once Shao and I went downtown", MacAdams recalled, "and just wrote what went down all day from the moment the sun went up to the moment the sun went down . . . there were years that went by where I was really happy just looking down at the ground and seeing what was growing . . . Bolinas was like the whole cosmos to me. You could do everything in Bolinas that you could do in New York City or Paris, on a mythological or cosmological level, and that was totally true for me at the time."

A PSYCHEDELIC PEYTON PLACE

In 1969 poet Ed Sanders dubbed Bolinas "a psychedelic Peyton Place". He wasn't far off the mark. *Peyton Place*, the 1956 novel by Grace Metalious, was a best-seller that was later made into a movie, spawning a television soap opera of the same name. The main plot follows the lives of three women, their personal travails and sexual awakenings, in a small New England town. The novel is notorious for its portrayal of the hypocrisy, social inequities, lust, incest, adultery, and murder that existed beneath the peaceful surface of the small town. The title "Peyton Place" became a common catchphrase to describe any place known for its "sordid atmosphere or nefarious doings."

While Bolinas wasn't quite as "sordid" there was an ongoing soap opera taking place, but one so involved and complicated as to be nearly impossible to unravel. As Duncan McNaughton said, "Everybody slept with everybody… it was charming, except when it was not charming, then it was really a drag." Suffice it to say that the chronology of "who was sleeping with who" is a separate history on its own. It was, after all, the height of the era of sex, drugs, and rock and roll, and this was a community that was largely formed of the members of that counterculture which had made "sex, drugs, and rock and roll" one of the iconic phrases of the time. Everything was called into question, from the place of women in society to the middle-class American ideals of marriage and monogamy. Similar "psychedelic Peyton Place's" could be found in San Francisco, New Yorks' lower east side, and countless other bohemian enclaves of the time. In the small community of Bolinas, the experimentation and seemingly restless liaisons were amplified.

The newest albums by artists such as the Grateful Dead, the Rolling Stones, Dylan, and Neil Young were greeted with much enthusiasm. There was considerable discussion of rock music among the poets, many of whom had poems printed in *Rolling Stone* magazine, which was still being published out of San Francisco at the time. Bill Berkson remembers dropping acid and spending an hour listening to Neil Young's *After the Gold Rush* on headphones until interrupted by a party of slide watchers led by Margot Doss.

Drug use cannot be discounted as an important part of life during this period in Bolinas. While this was largely a product of the era, daily tripping, whether on pot, hashish, LSD, mushrooms, or mescaline, was as much a part of the landscape as eucalyptus trees, nasturtiums and the Pacific Ocean.

Letters by the poets who lived there are full of accounts of dropping acid and wandering about the mesa, meeting other poets, talking, sitting down to write collaborations while drinking wine and smoking grass. To many, scoring pot was as essential as gathering firewood.

There were a lot of drugs flowing into Bolinas. Largely psychedelics of one kind or another. There weren't many hardcore drugs on the scene at the time—no heroin or cocaine (although the latter made a big time splash there in the late seventies). When Ted Berrigan stayed in Bolinas in the early seventies there was a flurry of amphetamine usage, speed being Berrigan's drug of choice. Lewis MacAdams remembered shooting speed with Berrigan in Bolinas.

‡

Bolinas attracted a wide variety of psychedelic refugees. Some were unfortunate burn-out cases with names like "No Memory" (an actual character in town who claimed to have washed up on the beach), others were just young, spaced-out hippies who lived in derelict cars or vans that were abandoned on the mesa. Their presence was an ongoing problem.

The Jefferson Airplane bought a house in Bolinas, all rigged-out with surveillance equipment in a very unBolinasian style, and they attracted all kinds of zonked-out fans. An article in *The Paper*, (April 8, 1972) by Gordon Baldwin, tells of a rainy night encounter with one of these hangers-on. The article, entitled "Stray Cat, or Lit Windows, a Liability", recounts how Baldwin was interrupted from working on a drawing early one evening by a knock on the door. A young guy, dripping wet, explained that he was, as Baldwin wrote, "waiting for the rock and roll stars who live across the street. He uses their first names only". He asks for shelter from the rain. Baldwin lets him in and asks, "What's your story?" The kid's story is a rambling account of traveling from Albany, New York to San Francisco in pursuit of rock stars. He's a guitar player and wants to talk to all his rock heroes. He was arrested at the Keystone Korner (a San Francisco music venue) for busting up a Garcia-Saunders session, he just wanted to "talk to Garcia, address the audience a little,'" he took forty doses of LSD in six months, etc. It becomes apparent that the kid has no intention to leave any time soon. Baldwin winds up giving him two dollars and telling him he should just hitchhike out of town. But the next morning, there he is again, leaning on the intercom at the Airplane house, and later trying to gain access to Baldwin's house as well. Baldwin mentions the encounter to some friends who say that they've seen the kid downtown bumming cigarettes. "What is it about this town that makes it possible for the strays to stay?", Baldwin asks. The kid was eventually arrested trying to vault the security fence at the Airplane house. Baldwin ends the article, "Hope the cat keeps out of town. Moral? Who polices whom? Where did our privacy go in flight from the new equality? And country hospitality to wayfaring strangers? As the song says, no place to run, no place to hide—from everything that's happening out there."

‡

"I took endless amounts of drugs when I was there," said Lewis Warsh, "and that tended to confuse and diffuse a lot of the emotional intensity that was further amplified by the presence of all the poets". Poet Lawrence Kearney said, "My own demons and my own isolation would keep me always from any group identification, and my raging alcoholism gave me the perfect out." While he spoke on a regular basis to poets such as John Thorpe, Duncan McNaughton, and Joanne Kyger, Kearney said that in Bolinas he "stayed reasonably apart, drank uncontrollably, and edged into madness."

During his tenure in Bolinas, Robert Creeley was drinking heavily, which added to the strain of his already shaky marital situation. Creeley told Jim Koller that his life in Bolinas was spent on the road between his house and the bar. He had been 86'd from the bar countless times.

The photo by Gerard Malanga on the cover of Creeley's *The Contexts of Poetry: Interviews 1961-1971* (Four Seasons Foundation, 1973) is an early morning shot of Creeley walking on a Bolinas road. He's looking at the camera with a wild smile, as though laughing, his hands held out in front of his body, fingers outstretched. The story behind this photo is that Creeley had been tripping all night with friends, wandering around the mesa.

It needs to be noted that Creeley was at the same time not only a major influential poet, but a very warm and generous man. Joanne Kyger recalled how many of the poets in town would visit Creeley when he returned from his numerous reading and teaching engagements. "We would just sit at his feet and listen to him as he gave us a report on what happened during his journeys," Kyger said. There was a deep respect for Creeley, especially among the poets. His marital troubles were largely kept private. Joe Brainard wrote in his *Bolinas Journal*, "Bob and Bobbie each exist individually so well. And together so well too." At the end of the book, listing all that he'll miss as he leaves Bolinas, Brainard adds, "And very sweet Bob. And very mysterious Bobbie." Most accounts of visitors to the Creeley home ring along similar lines, and yet Creeley himself was reticent in recounting his years in Bolinas. "It was a difficult time for me," he said.

"Creeley's intensities in were incredible!", said Tom Clark. When he was high, no matter what he happened to be high on, he became, as Clark said, "challenging and weird". At a big Fourth of July picnic celebration in the early seventies, Creeley had dropped acid, wrapped his head in tin foil and proceeded to terrify a young woman, chasing her off into the trees. On another occasion, recounted by Tom Clark, Creeley and he were walking on the mesa one night, accompanied by Creeley's dog, Spot. Creeley, who was on acid, began screaming lines from Olson's *Maximus from Dogtown* at the top of his lungs. He then turned to Clark and asked for a cigarette. Clark didn't have any cigarettes. They were on Elm Road and a car approached. Creeley stood in front of the car to stop it, leaned in the window and asked the car's occupants if anyone had a cigarette. Someone did, so Creeley climbed into the car with them and they all drove away leaving Clark and Spot standing on Elm Road. That night Spot went home with Clark.

The noble concept of permission within the community was, at times, tested. There was an unspoken code of tolerance for wildly different attitudes and permutations. It was understood on a very basic level. But there were casualties.

‡

Jack Boyce was always a serious drinker. He was living in his still unfinished house, which he was then sharing with Magda Cregg. One night in 1972, high, or drunk, or both, he decided to walk across one of the roof beams. He lost his balance, fell, and died. He had broken his neck.

Coming a year after Lew Welch took a revolver and walked away into the Sierra foothills above Gary Snyder's property to kill himself (his body was never found), an event that shocked and saddened many in Bolinas, the news of Boyce's death hit the community hard. Boyce was a great hero to so many—an artist, well-read, and very intelligent, but also a guy that could get things done. He had considerable skill as a carpenter, had lived in the backwoods, and had that easy, competent masculine demeanor of being able to do just about anything—all of which were highly prized in Bolinas. MacAdams said, "He was like my guru for a while, so I never really saw him the way other people did," adding, "but he was drinking a lot towards the end."

Boyce's ashes were scattered at a ceremony held on Mount Tamalpais. In his elegiac poem "Heart Photos", Lewis MacAdams writes:

> The ashes of Jack Boyce's body
> Will be consecrated to the Mountain
> Tamalpais at noon Monday
> at Mountain Theatre.
> "His spirit leads."

"They've got to be kidding," says Shao.

"They're not kidding," says woe.

Whatever the power source is, it burns
it does not dissolve.

Creeley felt an intense despair after Boyce's death. He said
that he recognized that, "My life was much the same."

A POET'S GHETTO

*Everybody was kind of aggressively being a poet,
and aggressively being everything else, in such a
heightened context.*

- Lewis MacAdams

The list of poets who were living in Bolinas, or just passing through, continued to grow as the seventies progressed. Joanne Kyger describes the attraction the town had:

Bolinas offered an alternative lifestyle, one that was sought at that time in the late 60s and early 70s. A small coastal town of about 500 inhabitants at the time, it offered rural living, the hippies versus the surfers for softball teams, and in large letters painted on the sea wall NEW YORK REFUGEES GO HOME…The pictures of those years have everyone sitting on the ground, shoulder high long grasses, and long hair. On Indian print bedspreads. We could sit all afternoon, with bottles of wine and smokes, and conversation and poetry, moving along with the path of the sun. Nobody sits on the ground anymore. Bolinas was a destination point.

Two important and influential newcomers to this destination point were Aram Saroyan and Duncan McNaughton, who both moved to town in 1972, and became long term residents.

Saroyan has said that living in Bolinas fundamentally redefined his sense of the role of a writer. His claim to fame as a poet was primarily fueled by the controversy over his extremely minimalist one-word poems. One of these one-word poems, "lighght", was chosen for a National Endowment of the Arts Poetry Award, and later would be used in attacks on what was argued to be wasteful use of NEA funding. Bolinas, Saroyan said, taught him to expand his artistic attentions from the strictly artistic creation of one-word "objects" to a sense of being a poet, attuned to artistic opportunities, but at the same time "tuned to a wavelength where art is secondary to life". "I began speaking as a citizen," he wrote in the Afterword to his book *Day & Night: Bolinas Poems* (Black Sparrow, 1998), "about all the things that were important to me: my wife, child, family, friends, and community … the psychic X-factor provided by Bolinas is exactly the sort of lightning one waits to be struck by. In one fell swoop, it provided a new chapter in my writing life."

The community that so impressed Saroyan upon his arrival in Bolinas was one that consisted of not only a great many of his literary colleagues but one in which people of his own age, background, and experience were "empowered." Bolinas was, Saroyan said "…very liberating, full of pitfalls, magical, and a bit maniacal."

"The same kinds of things that happened in Bolinas probably happened in Papua, New Guinea," said Tom Clark, "only all the centuries of anthropological tradition which were required to build up the customs and procedures in Papua, New Guinea, were all being created on the spot."

Lewis Warsh remembered that, "There was a lot of license—to be yourself, to go nuts, to fall in love, to be depressed and not see anyone for days, etc.—and a lots of support among ourselves, but there was also a feeling in the air that conspired against all the positive energy, and, as always, in all communities, it was the assertion of individual egos (who was strong, who was weak) that raised the intensity level beyond the point where I could stay there much longer than I did."

"So much vibrated out from Bolinas," said Anne Waldman, it was "the most intense collection of poets in one place not around an academic or university scene—so therefore more visionary, 'utopian'."

Poet Harris Schiff, who was an integral figure on the New York lower east side poetry scene, visited Bolinas often in the winter and spring of '69-'70 while living in San Francisco. Schiff told Warsh, "It's always good to know a place like Bolinas exists—even if you don't live in it" (quoted by Lewis Warsh in a letter to Bill Berkson, May 15 1970).

"It was a scene of intense concentration. A community," McNaughton said, "It hasn't anything to do with sentiment or agreement in values. It has to do with sympathetic coexistence in a single human fabric...We were, many of us, living together, and that makes some deeper human sympathies possible. There was no agreement at all, except the one of permission. That is a very subtle matter and asks a thoughtful inspection." The essential humanity of the town was remarkable. As McNaughton put it, "It was a way of life, one was on duty all the time." Within this context of permission the discipline was somewhat strange and it took some a few years to understand it. Others never really did.

‡

The motive force in Bolinas (to paraphrase Roger Shattuck's description of the avant-garde in turn-of-the-century Paris) came from individuals reacting to each other and occasionally discovering a common end, yet never surrendering their integrity. They remained individuals, whom only critics and enemies lumped together, in order to have a bigger target.

To some outsiders it seemed like an incestuous scene. A San Francisco poet dubbed it "a poet's ghetto." Others dismissed Bolinas poets as "zonked-out bucolics" or "lobotomized Fielding Dawson-types."

The place in general was seen as nothing more than "an asylum run by the inmates," as one frustrated member of the Marin County Board of Supervisors claimed. Saroyan recalls that, "Someone once said to me: 'It's very difficult to identify the lunatic fringe in Bolinas'."

But most of those who lived there obviously had a different viewpoint. "It was a literate population," said McNaughton, "there was a strong feeling for the presence of poetry and poets. It mattered, unlike elsewhere. The poets were held in esteem—an extension of the unusual acknowledgement of poets for a long time in San

Francisco. Not that poets couldn't be assholes—just that there was respect for the poem."

‡

The Berkeley Poetry Conference (July 12-24, 1965) can be seen as a precursor to the gathering of poetries that occurred in Bolinas, and there are many connections between that event and the community of poets at Bolinas, on many different levels.

One of the watershed events in the world of poetry, the Berkeley Poetry Conference was organized by Richard Baker in conjunction with the U.C. Berkeley Extension. Baker, who later was appointed abbot of the San Francisco Zen Center, also organized a conference on LSD the following year. The Berkeley Poetry Conference, structured around Donald Allen's seminal anthology *The New American Poetry: 1945-1960*, featured contributors to that anthology, such as Charles Olson, Robert Creeley, Jack Spicer, Robert Duncan, Allen Ginsberg, Ed Dorn, Lew Welch, and Gary Snyder. Other poets who read at the event were Joanne Kyger, Ed Sanders, Jim Brodey, and Ted Berrigan.

This was a major gathering of poets and hundreds of people attended. As in the Allen anthology, the several, divergent "schools" of American poetry were represented—Black Mountain, Beat, New York—just as they were to be in Bolinas as great number of these poets eventually visited or lived in Bolinas, even Donald Allen himself moved there.

Jim Koller and Bill Brown published a transcription of Charles Olson's controversial appearance at the conference as one of their Coyote Books in 1966. Olson's presentation was viewed by some as a monumental nuclear meltdown, and by others as a triumph. As Anne Waldman, who was in the audience at the time, remembers:

> I took a further vow to poetry at the Charles Olson marathon event, for he read and spoke and raged and wept more than he technically "read". But Olson was powerful that night, vulnerable, arrogant, bombastic, poignant, embarrassing. He was the poet coming apart before our eyes, scapegoat, shaman, doing it for us.... His friends were dismayed....

53

Something very Bolinasian in Waldman's take on Olson's performance, "the poet coming apart before our eyes", "doing it for us", rhyming as it does with the concept of "permission" within the community, as Duncan McNaughton and others have pointed out. This permission was, however, something more than merely tolerance.

‡

Was there a Bolinas poetic? Duncan McNaughton said, "What poets did there was their business." While it could be argued that there was no single shared aesthetic, other than the poet's personal engagement with the poem, there were distinct elements in Bolinas poetry that were common and invite a closer consideration.

Any attempt to label or categorize the rich subtleties and multilayered variances inherent in, not just Bolinas poetry, but all poetry in general, is a bad habit promulgated by academics and critics. The designations of Black Mountain, New York School, Beat and San Francisco Renaissance should be considered as a kind of shorthand for those who may not be familiar with the individual poets discussed. To characterize the poetry written by a group of poets who shared similar motivations and aesthetics, in subtle often complicated ways, within the context of a specific time and place, is a textual challenge that does not necessarily lead to a neatly labeled package. However, there would seem to be compelling evidence that among the poets of Bolinas there were common aesthetic threads, and that these threads were ultimately woven into the poetry written there.

A Bolinas poetic could be understood as a synthesis of the poetries represented in Donald Allen's *The New American Poetry* anthology. Donald Allen was an inspired editor, from his work at Grove Press, and his editorship of the *Evergreen Review* in the 1950s, to the publication of his landmark anthology in 1960, he championed the work of the non- academic, underground poets who were writing some of the most important works of the era. When he moved to San Francisco in the sixties he established his Four Seasons Foundation which went on to publish Richard Brautigan's novels and poetry, along with books by Gary Snyder, Philip Whalen, Joanne Kyger, Robert Creeley, and many others. Allen was appointed literary executor for Frank O'Hara and compiled *The Collected Poems of Frank O'Hara* which was published by Knopf in 1971. He was also the literary executor for Lew Welch, and published *Ring of Bone: The Collected Poems of Lew Welch* under his own Grey Fox Press imprint. His presence in Bolinas was significant and he was greatly respected by all.

The *New American Poetry* anthology presented an alternative tradition in American poetry, one that had been ignored by academics and critics alike. Allen structured the anthology around the several distinct "schools" within the sub radar poetries of the time. These distinctions were to be blurred, if not erased altogether, by the Bolinas poets.

It is interesting to note that of the forty-four poets that were included in the Allen anthology thirteen were either visitors to or residents of Bolinas.

A major influence upon Bolinas poetry was Charles Olson. Olson, who had the important position of being the lead-off poet in Allen's anthology, had numerous connections to the poets of Bolinas. As stated earlier, Donald Allen's anthology as played out on the stage of the Berkeley Poetry Conference, could be viewed as a sneak preview of the gathering of poets in Bolinas. Koller and Brown's Coyote Books publication of Olson's famous (or infamous) presentation at the conference, was published shortly before the two moved to Bolinas. Robert Duncan, who taught at Black Mountain and was a close friend of Olson's, later served as a mentor to Joanne Kyger and Lawrence Kearny, as well as to Ebbe Borregaard who had also spent time with Olson at Black Mountain in the fifties.

Olson himself visited Bolinas in 1968. Joanne Kyger, who at the time was working in experimental television at the San Francisco PBS station, arranged for Olson to be filmed reading his poetry for television. While Olson was in San Francisco Kyger and Jack Boyce drove him up to Bolinas to spend the day visiting Bill Brown. Kyger remembered that Olson had a vigorous, animated discussion with Hal Chase about boatbuilding.

John Clarke taught Olson's Myth and Literature course at Buffalo in the mid-sixties. Among his students were Lewis MacAdams and Duncan McNaughton. Clarke also oversaw the Curriculum of the Soul series of fascicles—seven of which were written by poets with Bolinas connections—Lewis MacAdams,

Duncan McNaughton, Joanne Kyger, Jim Koller, John Thorpe, Robert Grenier, and John Clarke. Clarke's contribution being the aforementioned mythologized treatment of Bolinas poets in the form of a Blakean prophesy.

With the arrival of Robert Creeley in Bolinas the connection to Olson was hardwired. Creeley was a direct link and as his poetry was affected by Bolinas so were the poets there affected by the confluence of practice and process, life and text, that he brought with him. In this context, the image of Creeley, high on acid, screaming lines from Olson's *Maximus from Dogtown* on the Bolinas mesa, takes on a mythic quality all its own.

Olson's influence is to be noted as well among the younger poets that emerged from the News York's lower east side. Lewis Warsh early on had a deep interest in Olson and the Black Mountain poets:

> These poets taught me that psychology, magic, history, and dailiness could exist in poetry in equal measure. The New York School poets sounded a bit too formal and rhetorical to me, too on the surface—
> (Lewis Warsh, *The Angel Hair Anthology*)

Olson's theory of Projective Verse— "A poem is energy transferred from where the poet got it (he will have some several causations), by way of the poem itself to, all the way over to, the reader. . . the poem itself must, at all points, be a high energy-construct and, at all points, an energy-discharge... ONE PERCEPTION MUST IMMEDIATELY AND DIRECTLY LEAD TO A FURTHER PERCEPTION"—had a notable impact among poets on the lower east side scene. Anne Waldman has said that "Olson was the father of us all."

The hallmarks of Bolinas poetry include an engagement with everyday mystery, with social critique and transcendence set against the imagery of the place within the context of the community, as factors in a very "human universe". And along those lines confronting the place, in particular and general, and where that leads one, inside and out, is a direct offshoot from Olson's teachings.

Olson throws down a long shadow, but it is really in the mix of poetries that one can begin to understand and describe a Bolinas poetic. The dailiness and "personism" of New York poets such as Frank O'Hara were also in play. Bill Berkson, who had spent a considerable amount of time with O'Hara was an important link. The spirit of poetic collaboration that came out of the St. Mark's scene was continued in Bolinas, notably by Tom Clark, Lewis Warsh, Ted Berrigan, and Lewis MacAdams. Creeley's *In London* shows the influence of the New York School—possibly because of Creeley's close contact with Ted Berrigan during the time those poems were written. The use of humor which characterized not only New York School, but Beat poetry as well, became an integral part of Bolinas poetry, as did references to Buddhist and Eastern philosophy (an aspect of Beat poetry, particularly that which was written out of the San Francisco North Beach scene, as emblematic of a West Coast aesthetic).

The occultism and alchemy of the Duncan-Spicer circle, as well as the Buddhist "dharma bum" and Native American influences that came through the poetry of Gary Snyder, Lew Welch, and Philip Whalen, were also important influences that informed Bolinas poetry. The latter three poets had attended Reed College in Oregon together, and all later relocated to San Francisco. Snyder was a counterculture hero, for his poetry and radical eco-politics as much as for the notoriety provided by Jack Kerouac's portrayal of him as Japhy Ryder in *The Dharma Bums*—a novel that portrayed a back-to-nature movement and lifestyle that 15 years later would be an important aspect of the hippie counterculture.

Welch was a formidable presence on the San Francisco scene during the late sixties. He became involved with the Diggers and taught a poetry workshop for the UC Berkeley Extension. His readings were extraordinary events and his poetry was very important to many of the Bolinas poets. The refrain from his poem "The Song Mt. Tamalpais Sing"—"This is the last place. There is nowhere else to go"—was appropriated by the Bolinas Future Studies Center for use as the title of one section of the Marin County Bolinas Plan. Whalen's characterization of his own poetry as "a picture or graph of a mind moving, which is a world body being here and now which is history . . . and you", encompasses day to day perception, subjective phenomena, fleeting thoughts and attentions, along with a free use of references from a prodigious reading list in Eastern, primarily Buddhist, literature, the classics, and poetry from the Greek Anthology to Allen Ginsberg. It is a dazzlingly rich, funny and open poetic score that had a major effect upon the Bolinas poets, most of whom Whalen had close and lasting relationships with.

The fusion of these diverse yet concurrent approaches to the poem provide a loose frame of reference for the poetry of Bolinas. Flexible enough to expand and contract, as the poems themselves do. This 1967 journal entry by Joanne Kyger can, to varying degrees, be read as the underlying theory and practice of Bolinas poetry:

> The structure of poetry interests me. All its layers. I do not like to see one image worked upon and developed, unless of course it is very insistent; but to see the stray and often extraneous seeming bits of image and fact brought to bear upon a loosely scattered area which is the poem. The linear aspect of the poem being merely a suggested voice line to take you from the beginning to the end, but suggesting no such consecutiveness in thought. The area of the poem is able to contain all elements. For what one can recognize and adhere to is the continuity, no matter how or where it comes from.

‡

Robert Creeley has said that being in Bolinas made him want to get out of some of his internal emotional rhetoric and try to confront the place. "I want to walk around here," he wrote in his poem "Bolinas and Me":

> look at the people, pretty,
> look at the houses, stop in
> the bar, get the mail, get
> going again, somewhere.
> ....
> The liquor store lights
> shine out in the night,
> and one is walking, going,
> coming, in the night.

Holy place we stand in,
these changes—

Creeley learned from Bolinas. The poems in his book *Thirty Things*, (Black Sparrow Press, 1974), for example, are small but they have an absence of preconceptions and emotional structures that is a marked change in his poetry:

As You Come
As you come down
the road, it swings
slowly left and the sea
opens below you,
west. It sounds out.

No
No farther out
than in—
no nearer here
than there.

Here
Here is
where there
is.

Xmas Poem: Bolinas
All around
the snow
don't fall.
Come Christmas
we'll get high
and go find it.

Photo
       for Joanne
They say a
woman passes at

the edge of the
house, turning
the corner, leaves
a very vivid sense,
after her
of having been there.

Similarly, the short poems in Saroyan's *The Bolinas Book*
(Other Publications, 1974), speak in a straightforward, deceptively
simple language, directly to the people and the place:

THE BOLINAS SCENE (1)
It's interesting living in a community
Of people you know rather intimately
You can tell a lot from body posture
Or the fog in the air, what is going on here
There are a few birds
But many more stars on clear nights

THE BOLINAS SCENE (2)
Who am I?
Who are you?
Who is Lewis?
Who is Joanne?
And where is
Michael McClure?

ROBERT CREELEY
Robert Creeley
is a town figure
of no small
dimension.

THE BOLINAS SCENE (5)
Getting yourself
operated on
by Bolinas, California—
all your friends there,
good doctors & nurses.

JOANNE KYGER'S WRITING DESK
Joanne Kyger's writing desk
doesn't exist.

TOM CLARK
I come over
Find you listening to The Beach Boys
With headphones.

LEWIS MACADAMS, JR.
The best
basket-ball-
player in town
is Lewis MacAdams, Jr.

Snapshots of Bolinas can be found in so many of the poems written there, each with their own unique framing and composition. Bill Berkson's poem "Twilight Time" contains the following list of Bolinas street names, tracing the route he walks to the Clark home on Nymph Road:

>...& walking
> along on straight, starlit roads:
> Brighton, Terrace, Ocean Parkway, Grove
> & Juniper, Kale,
> Laurel, Maple, & on
> down Cherry, a little ways up Nymph
> here to there
> the days are endless
> though they surely go...

Poet and photographer Gerard Malanga, an early player at Andy Warhol's Factory in New York, and an important link between Warhol and the St. Mark's poets, lived in Bolinas for several months in 1973. While in Bolinas he snapped portraits of many of the poets and wrote several poetic portraits of the place, such as this quick polaroid entitled "10:00 pm Bolinas":

the only thing happening
is the ocean
outside this window

Malanga also contributed his own version of "Things to do in Bolinas":

wake up
go back to sleep
wake up again
wash face
brush teeth
asanas
mantra yoga
tea with honey
water the plants
write this mornings poem
read book
correspondence
phone don allen
laundry
visit friends
exchange poems
take photos
karma yoga
talk to flowers animals birds
climb hill
see the sun
thank the boss for everything
go to the post office
that there may be some news from you

Tom Clark adds to this poetry of dailiness, as in these samples from his poem "A Sailor's Life":

You're a piece
of the same person
I'm a piece of.

*

Who is Lewis?
Who is Joanne?

*

What'd Ed Sanders
call Bolinas—
a psychedelic
Peyton Place?

*

Visitors
in 1969:
too many
to name.

*

After the rain
camellias
bloom too soon.

*

half silver
half black
eucalyptus leaf

*

follow the downstream flow
to the store—difficult
hitchhiking—the winter
of Charles Manson

*

A place where
the time of the year
is a color—
dark green

To capture Olson's directive "ONE PERCEPTION MUST
IMMEDIATELY AND DIRECTLY LEAD TO A FURTHER
PERCEPTION" is to understand that poetry is continually
revelatory. What it reveals is the everyday world in which the poet
dwells.

I say
this is real this is true there
I am
walking
down the road.
Then there's a sense
of senses in a circle just
where they should be, that if
there's that real that bright
the haze and the clearness
have their real worlds their
invisible chested
blue plane people
walking past me like surfaces
the trees reflect in.
　　　(Lawrence Kearney, from *Songs*)

Again and again in the poems one finds that particular
dailiness and attention to the immediate world that surrounds one:

It's a green uprising of weed & clover
grass spears reaching higher each season
out of ground we tried to till but found
useless for want of constant sunlight
The light speaks thru green leaves…
　　　(David Meltzer, "From: Sefer Ha-Adam")

A conversation rather than a confrontation with the place, as in this sonnet by Ebbe Borregaard:

MY BOLINAS

I am all that aspirations will contend
you, young of the east westward wending
It is for you I have been loved over & over
In alien temples, in homefields, where I was a rover
We have waited since the first celestial dawn
yr lovelyness to meet, the power of our Loving
as the principle law this univers abides
We luckt in its size & within us it is hiding
And I have waited out all my unthinking days
for yr glad light inbreathing, inothering my ways
As I tript on roots of misery & ate leaves of despair
looting the Stars for yr incandescent hair
See all the continuum knows the Cosmic Folly
which wld allow the human Ebbe no Angelic Dolly.
    (Ebbe Borregaard, from *27 Songs*)

In Max Crosley's "Epic Today", the poet details a chronicle of a day in Bolinas that works both from the inside out, and the outside in:

A black and ochre-fuzzed bee hovers and lands on the
flower of a weed as I'm out of the house, down to the end
of the road. Having paid my dues, I now live and walk in
an unurban world where the bees continue to collect pollen
and I can make all the word honey I try, here, now, on this
path, down the cliffs off the mesa, to the sea

…the tide's in and the beach diminished…white foam up to
my feet as I pause to write…it just keeps coming…ankle
bent on the rocks…the cliffs falling…it keeps coming with
its dirty angry waste shaped motion…hear the birds
faintly…but here, always the rhythm to keen up the ears…

Turn off the beach, silence downtown…pick a nasturtium, eat it (remembering e.e. cummings directive, ''perhaps it is better to eat flowers and not be afraid'')…tart cabbage taste…raw burning in the back of the mouth…take care of business…mail, pick it up…groceries, pick 'em up…eat another nasturtium…burn, baby, burn…surfers and young girls going to the beach…

----

a crow awkwardly walks down the driveway beside the restaurant, between bushes of roses, through the roof and into the air, cawing Smiley's, Snarley's, Scowley's…many songs…

In his poem "To Greene Street", Lewis MacAdams gives his take of Bolinas as a fabled refuge, part of one's destiny, in a mythic sense:

> … There is a place
> we can go to be well and act well, but sometimes
> to get there we've got to kill somebody and then we've got
> to go there all alone. I'm there now, and Agate Beach
> tumbles with her moonstones. Sometimes
> the whole continent trembles…

The underlying mythic dimensions of the place and time, something that poets are particularly attuned to, shows again in a poem by Berkson. It's a short poem but it packs enough to fill a novel:

> *A-FRAME*
> air blue
> ocean plain
> & glowing
> baby sleeping
> woman turning
> man on fire

Like a mirror, a shattered mirror, each poet reflected his or her own separate perception of Bolinas. Duncan McNaughton's poem "Bolinas", from his book *Shit On My Shoes* (Tombouctou, 1979), is a poem about marriage, although these lines would seem to offer a particularly concise, distilled, and perceptive evaluation of the rigorous expectations within the community of Bolinas:

> compulsion superseded by orders
> yawning emptiness by service
> resolute solitude by confirmation
> adversity by purpose

What is offered by the poetry of Bolinas is, to use a quote from Robert Creeley, "the sense that poetry isn't a discretion, that it is ultimately the realization of an entire world."

In *The Cargo Cult* (Big Sky, 1972), John Thorpe embraces Bolinas much as Charles Olson did Gloucester:

>   . . . I address Bolinas
> as if it were a condition
> to be occupied
>   as if it Arose
> not after Frisco that monsoon of lights
> but rather the unclaimed silt beach of
> phonepoles, bridges, houses, shoes—a last outpost takes
> out here, and the rest of the world a wake
> of minor shocks not for a moment
>   to be received as
> history
>   except of delay
> or the question can a 'town' afford
> to have lived less
> than the men
>   she
> fosters

Thorpe's remarkable range and command is apparent everywhere in his poetry, from the use of early investigative historical data on Bolinas, to the direct biography of his consciousness as laid out in a poem like "I Just Lost My Tension

Again", which lists the attributes and the defects inherent in the condition of his existence:

> There's a man in me who would prove. He is right but little else.

The separation between those two sentences alters the meaning, slightly, like a skip in a recording. Thorpe continues in a confessional mode, "I blew money. I lost things", and adds, "I feel like everyone knows me"—perhaps suggesting that either they don't really know him, or that perhaps they are the only ones who do know him, or that he actually doesn't even know himself? But Thorpe recovers:

> There's a laugh which indicates simply I drink and I'm too afraid to pay attention.

The self-deprecating tone that carries the narrative of the poem is turned into a kind of nobility suggesting nothing less than triumph in the closing lines:

> I did very little. I had a central character by virtue of that. Not as if I'd found a place they couldn't take away.

> I did what I wanted. And I brought two children into this world. I respected the mystery and mastered nothing I'm aware of.

> I squat here, looking at the moon, deciding to appear.

The conscious placement of the poet within the community, a particularly Bolinasian concern, finds it's mythological split when a poem like "I Just Lost My Tension Again" is read alongside another small masterpiece by Thorpe:

> If anyone says I live in a town
> The sea is my order
> I know sheet water
> & when so, it's been

coast, I am no damn
good for depth
    (like bowels
rightly beyond that
dip at the end of the
beach before I stand
      deep
    waves come
up to be pulled over very quickly very
cold, in, dense, I go back
Oh
     what tricks did Mars try
     before and the air is so
     much wind you shout, lost

Joanne Kyger's poetry reads as part dream journal, part daybook, while displaying a truly astounding depth and range. There seems on the surface to be a simple, easy flow that sustains her line, but there is more than that. As Kyger has written, it's "the part of the writer that stays alive while 'personality' seems to be more and more a dried-up appendage of 'identity'. The 'individual' is swept out to sea, a group location identity, a place, takes precedence as voice." The "place" in her poems is most often Bolinas. Her method, then, could be given in these lines from *All This Every Day* (Big Sky, 1975):

    I tell my complaints.
    I intricately recite the details of the day and the
    possibilities of what they mean

Kyger notes the people, and the place, the natural world, and its ongoing conversations in way that is both intimate and private, while also standing somewhere to the side, objectively observing:

    Watching everything, everything happens. Inside the pace,
    well, it's rhythm & pulse too, you meet others inside
    this flow, of the day, the whole town moves, meeting
    across each other, traveling for a while.

(from "RCA Beach and Arthur Okamura" in *All This Every Day*)

It would seem that there is nothing at all certain in the sweep of time, except that she is in it:

> when I invoke the moon
>> it's the best I can find
> and all of Bolinas
>> at my feet

The poem above is from her book *Joanne*, (Angel Hair, 1970), described as "a novel from the inside out." It's a Bolinas book in its locale, its sensibilities, and its inside-out references and sympathies:

> what I wanted to say
>> was in the broad
> sweeping
> form of being there
> I am walking up the path
> I come home and wash my hair
>> I am bereft
> I dissolve quickly
> I am everybody

With so many poets living in close quarters there were many collaborative poems being written. Like *Bolinas Eyewash* by Berrigan and Clark, several of these collaborations included Bolinas references, whether directly or implied:

> An Indian is
> better than
> a newspaper.
> If you want obedience
> piss on the rug first.
> The benefit of the
> doubt has engines.

The only way to
make money in
Bolinas is to
sell out.

        (John Thorpe & Ebbe Borregaard,
        from "Friday Night Proverbs by Shao & Ebbe",
        published in *The Paper*, #7, Nov. 15, 1971}

No more poems about inner nature
slimey or rambunctious, pure
I can't stand it
don't trust Aristotle (Ethics)
intellectual clarity I suspect
of capitalism
        a great guy wearing a bathrobe over a Levi
jacket

        (Bill Berkson and Joanne Kyger,
        untitled collaboration,
        published in *Big Sky*, Number Five, 1973)

Our Town

Faded army blankets stretched over the tops of
some huge fallen eucalyptus trunks
might not sound like much of a house
unless you arc from the outskirts of Rabat
but that's how we live in Bolinas.
What we call a Condo's three or four wrecked chevrolets
strung out along a dirt road.
We live in palaces constructed of mud
where it's so quiet you can hear the rats
piss on Kleenex.

        (from *Expeditions by Lewis & Clark* - Lewis
MacAdams & Tom Clark, unpublished manuscript, 1972)

A very beautiful collaboration between Gordon Baldwin and
Joanne Kyger was published as a small book entitled *Trip Out &*

Fall Back (Arif Press, 1975). Baldwin remembered that Kyger said "You draw the East, and I'll write about it." He did a series of drawings, and gave them to Kyger, who used the drawings as inspiration for her words:

> The vibes are too high
> They're Empire State high
> I'm a ground hole watcher
> Out my Bolinas window

Kyger and Lewis MacAdams collaborated on several plays for various civic events. Probably one of the most noteworthy of these was the play they wrote and performed at the opening of the sewer ponds. The Kyger/MacAdams performance included breaking a champagne bottle over a toilet.

There was another celebration round this time, for the dedication of a new park in town. The park was on the site of the Tarantino Seafood restaurant which burned down in 1974. When the debris had been cleared away the townspeople had various opinions as to what should be done with the vacant lot. It had been called People's Park, Tarantino's Park, and Burnt Park. When the decision was finally made to officially dedicate the park it was to be called Birth Park. During his performance, MacAdams, wearing goggle-like Adam Ant sunglasses, dropped to his knees in what appeared to be a shamanistic trance and began to eat dirt. As MacAdams explained, this performance piece was about giving life to the dead, eating the dead dirt symbolizing the transformance of life, as Burnt Park became Birth Park. The performance was appalling to some, poetic and memorable to others.

BIG SKY & CO.

As to be expected, several little literary magazines came out of the Bolinas scene. The first of these was a one-shot mimeo magazine edited by Lewis Warsh and Tom Clark in August of 1970 titled *Sugar Mountain*. Named after the Neil Young song the magazine featured a photograph by Jayne Nodland on the front and back cover of poet Alice Notley, nude, sitting on a couch looking directly into the camera (which angered Berrigan and Notley, since neither Warsh nor Clark had bothered to ask permission to use the photo). *Sugar Mountain* was printed on legal size paper and looked very much like a mimeo mag out of New York's lower east side. The magazine printed works by Bill Berkson, Ted Berrigan, Tom Clark, Scott Cohen, Clark Coolidge, Joanne Kyger, Lewis MacAdams, Alice Notley, Ron Padgett, Harris Schiff, John Thorpe, Charlie Vermont, Anne Waldman, and Lewis Warsh.

Warsh and Waldman had published *Angel Hair* in New York, but the magazine came to an abrupt end when they separated. However, they continued to publish Angel Hair books; Waldman from New York, and Warsh from Bolinas. Some of the Angel Hair books that Warsh published during his brief stay in Bolinas include *Chicago*, a collaboration by Warsh and Tom Clark, *In London* by Robert Creeley, *Joanne* by Joanne Kyger, and *Neil Young* by Tom Clark.

Similarly, Duncan McNaughton brought his magazine *Fathar,* which he started in June 1970 in Buffalo, New York, along with him to Bolinas where he published the final two issues in September 1974 and March 1975.

In 1971 Bill Berkson began publishing his magazine *Big Sky*. Carrying a healthy sampling of works by Bolinas writers, *Big Sky* also included poems from a number of important poets living outside of Bolinas. The first issue had a cover drawn by Greg Irons and inside printed Irons' cartoon "The Creature from Bolinas Lagoon" which was reprinted in *The Paper*. The issue also included works by Alice Notley, Ted Berrigan, Robert Creeley, Harris Schiff, Tom Veitch, Lewis Warsh, Diane di Prima, Tom Clark, Anne Waldman, Lewis MacAdams, Joanne Kyger, John Thorpe, Bobbie Creeley (Bobbie Louise Hawkins), Joe Brainard, Philip Whalen, Allen Ginsberg, and others. Subsequent issues had covers by Joe Brainard, Philip Guston, Gordon Baldwin, Geroge Schneeman, Norman Bluhm, Red Grooms, and Alex Katz.

The magazine's name was suggested by Tom Veitch who, as Berkson remembered "reminded me of the line from a Kinks song, 'Big Sky looks down on all the people'." Berkson's original editorial stance was to accept "whatever arrived from those invited to contribute." After the first two issues he found this method too "chaotic" and devoted the third issue entirely to work by Clark Coolidge. Thereafter he became a more selective editor. *Big Sky* had a run of 12 issues from 1971 to 1978 and was one of the most consistently sharp and loaded literary magazines to come out of Bolinas.

In addition to the magazine, Berkson also published a series of 20 Big Sky Books. Among these were *Bolinas Journal* by Joe Brainard, *All This Every Day* by Joanne Kyger, *The Cargo Cult* by John Thorpe, *Death Collage and Other Poems* by Tom Veitch, and Berkson's own *Enigma Variations*.

While most of the Big Sky publications were printed at The West Coast Print Center in Berkeley, the first issues of the magazine were produced at a Bolinas community printing press, called The Mesa Press, which was run by Mickey Cummings. A number of little publishing ventures ranging from community newsletters, (such as *The Paper*), ecological tracts, local concert and event flyers and posters, as well as poetry chapbooks, found their way into print because of The Mesa Press and Mickey Cummings.

It was via The Mesa Press that Aram Saroyan and Russ Riviere put out two issues of an untitled magazine featuring works by locals only. Their editorial policy, in keeping with the town's anarcho-pacifist participatory democracy, was "print whatever you're given". The first issue was published in March and the second in April of 1973. The first page of the March issue carried the following statements by the two editors:

If we are a Community
we must consider objectives
If we are the Buddha
we must consider Objectives
Big Vision
Little Steps

R.R.

Russ Riviere and I started talking together
at Scowley's one morning and just sort of hatched
this one. Gathering the material was a way of
greeting people again after the long rains. Spring
is in the air, neighborliness in blossom...

A.S.

With the community in mind, Riviere and Saroyan gathered writings from the town poets, those who were well known as poets, as well as work by anyone else who gave them something. The cover drawing for the March issue was by Arthur Okamura, with poems by the usual suspects: Kyger, MacAdams, Berkson, Clark, Creeley, Ebbe Borregaard, David Meltzer, and John Thorpe. But the issue also included writings by other residents such as Greg Hewlett, Captain Spatula, Patrick Holland, Bill Beckman (a short marketing plug titled "Why Support *Beaulines*"), and an indignant letter by Orville Schell to a *California Living Magazine* journalist who trashed Bolinas in an article entitled "Can Bolinas Get It Together?". The second issue featured many of the same contributors as the first, including artwork and a poem by Magda Cregg (also known as the mother of rocker Huey Lewis), a rant on education by Ponderosa Pine (Keith Lampe), and an announcement by Ellen Sander and Susanna Acevedo that a "directory of community services" was being compiled and that citizens were encouraged to contribute to it. Inside the back cover was a reproduction of a Jack Boyce painting, with this attribution: "Back page by the ever-present Jack Boyce".

This magazine may have been the prototype for one of the town's most remarkable and enduring publications. Town butcher and sometime school bus driver, Michael Rafferty, had the genius to recognize that the editorial policy of the Saroyan/Riviere magazine—"print whatever you're given"—made more sense for a newspaper than for a literary magazine. In 1974 Rafferty founded the *Bolinas Hearsay News*.

HEARSAY

The first issue of *The Bolinas Daily Hearsay News* hit the street on Monday, February 30, 1974. A legal size, mimeographed, single sheet of paper, printed on both sides and hand lettered entirely by Michael Rafferty, it sold for ten cents. This first issue was reminiscent of *The Bolinas Hit* in the reporting of humorous, tall-tale-like tidbits of imaginary news. For example, these items in the section titled "Of Local Interest":

> * Al Flat and Regina Cortez had a baby yesterday (their twelfth) & a 4 pound 6 ounce hermaphrodite! Needless to say, they hired neither doctor nor midwife. Al bit the cord with his teeth.

> * A cow exploded in flames last night in Sherman Smith's pasture, just as the full moon reached the zenith. Ikon saw this and swears it's true.

In the "Violence and Crime" section were three items of note:

> * Rocky got drunk and beat up Diana.

> * Robert Creeley was 86'd from the bar again for dinging the pool table light.

> * A car ran over Tamarra's left big toe last night on Wharf Road.

The first issue signs off with the note, "SEND US YOUR NEWS BY 6:00 P.M.—READ IT IN THE BOLINAS DAILY

HEARSAY NEWS THE NEXT MORNING". After the inaugural week the *Daily Hearsay*, became simply *The Bolinas Hearsay News*, and thereafter was published three times a week, Monday, Wednesday and Friday, with three separate editorial staffs for each day.

Joanne Kyger and Lewis MacAdams helped edit the Monday paper. As MacAdams remembered, "Joanne and I would come in at 10:30 on Monday morning to the *Hearsay* office and start drinking brandy and coffee and smoking joints and just waiting for people to come in and tell us what happened over the weekend, and we'd type it up. It was great! It was really fun. We'd get completely smashed and make like $20 apiece for the morning's work. We'd wrap up the paper by 1:00 and it'd be everywhere in Bolinas by 5 or 6."

The November 12, 1975, issue contained the following notice:

HEARSAY NEWS SOLICITS…
WRITERS, POETS, CARTOONISTS,
ARTISTS, SOCIETY COLUMNISTS, AND
ANYONE ELSE CAPABLE OF LEGIBILITY.
WE NEED AND APPRECIATE YOU…!
AND, TO A FEW OF OUR DEADBEAT
CRITICS…IF YOU DON'T LIKE WHAT YOU
READ…WRITE SOMETHING ELSE

This was essentially the editorial policy (and is to this day)— the people of Bolinas supplied the stories, either mailing them in or dropping them off at the *Hearsay* office. The editorial staff assembled the stories, ads, etc., creating a paste-up master copy which was handed off to Mickey Cummings at the Mesa Press to print. The only requirement of the items submitted by the community was that they be signed—no anonymous contributions were accepted.

The *Hearsay* was a lively mix of community news, social commentary, and gossip. The news supplied to the *Hearsay* from the community included poems, recipes, gardening tips, tide charts, short stories, astrology, cartoons, ads, reviews of books, movies, local performances and concerts, along with reports from the BPUD meetings, school board meetings, Bolinas Planning Commission, and Bolinas Property Owners Association. There was a regular "Alternative Sports" column by Greg Fontan (under the psuedonym of Herb Coon, a play on the name of the San Francisco Chronicle columnist Herb Caen). Coon's column was as much an account of the often hysterically funny escapades of Coon as it was a report of local baseball, basketball, soccer, and football games. Another fairly regular feature for a few years in the mid-seventies was a satirical advice column called "Ask Walter". Walter was actually Lawrence Kearney, and sometimes Annie Lamott. The "Ask Walter" column became a source of a spirited, often mean-spirited, debate. There was a decidedly snide and rude tone to the column that many in the community took issue with.

The *Hearsay* was not simply a newspaper, it was in many ways a community forum. Every community concern was addressed, and inevitably debated, by the citizens in the pages of the *Hearsay*. In the first few years of its existence there were ongoing debates on such issues as the water moratorium, the Bolinas dogs, proposals to move the Bolinas School, nudity on Bolinas beach, vagrants and crazies downtown, and whether or not Bill Niman should receive a permit to raise hogs on the mesa. There seemed to be no way to have a consensus on ANYTHING in Bolinas. There was a myriad of conflicting viewpoints, most of which found their way into print via the *Hearsay*.

An ongoing biography of the town, a true and immediate diary of community consciousness, *The Hearsay News* is still an important part of life in Bolinas. As Saroyan said, "The real story of Bolinas is contained in the pages of *The Hearsay News*."

JUST USING THE LANDSCAPE

In the early seventies Richard Brautigan bought the house on the mesa that the Meltzer's had been renting. Brautigan had become very famous and successful as a writer by this time. His novels, such as *Trout Fishing in America*, *A Confederate General at Big Sur*, and *In Watermelon Sugar* were noted for their dark, elegiac portrayal of human relationships along with a light, humorous, often fantastic and magical transformation of everyday phenomena, all in a very simple (some say naïve) direct prose. His books could be found in dorm rooms across the country. He was immensely popular among the counterculture in the sixties and his photograph was often featured on the covers of his books (usually depicting him in the company of a beautiful young hippie chick). Brautigan was an iconic figure and often boasted during this period of celebrity that he could step out on any highway and get a ride in minutes since everyone recognized him. He was also a deeply odd guy, who drank a lot, and was essentially a loner. Brautigan never stayed for long periods in Bolinas, showing up only occasionally, usually to briefly visit friends there, Robert Creeley and Joanne Kyger in particular.

Lawrence Ferlinghetti, like Brautigan, also bought a house in Bolinas but rarely spent any time there.

Writer Dale Herd first visited Bolinas in the early seventies to visit Don Allen. He later rented a long room in Susi Whaley's barn which was where he wrote his novel *Dreamland Court*, tacking up the pages on a long wall. In 1975 he rented a cottage from Bobbie Louise Hawkins that was on a small ridge behind her house on Terrace Avenue. But Herd was on the move a lot in those days. In 1979-80 when Michael Wolfe was preparing Herd's book *Wild Cherries* for publication by Tombouctou, Herd again rented the long room in Whaley's barn.

Another poet in town at this time was Jim Gustafson. Gustafson was friends with Andrei Codrescu and it was Codrescu who introduced Gustafson to Bolinas. As Berkson remembered, "Gustafson was a wild, nervous, huggy, committed writer, worked as a bartender at Smiley's, could jump the bar, like they say, and throw a guy out the swinging doors." His book *Tales of Virtue and Transformation* was published by Big Sky in 1974 with a cover by Greg Irons.

When Jim Carroll moved to Bolinas in 1973, he was "damaged goods". Years of heroin addiction had taken their toll. He enrolled in the methadone clinic in San Rafael (Bill Berkson drove him over the hill once a week) and settled into Bolinas, at first sharing a room with Jim Gustafson and Sara Schrom at the Grand Hotel, before moving to a little cottage, in the midst of a dense grove of eucalyptus trees, at the intersection of Mesa Road and Bolinas-Olema Road.

"I lived in total seclusion," Carroll said in a 1980 interview in *The San Francisco Review of Books,* "I'd just walk my dog every day for 12 miles, around Bolinas, Point Reyes." MacAdams recalled that "Jim lived the most isolate existence . . . most people when they think of Jim Carroll in Bolinas, it's like this spectral person in a serape, with his dog, Jo-mama, and carrying a big staff, some big long stick."

When he wasn't out on long hikes with his dog, Carroll stayed indoors and watched television, drank methadone, smoked, and wrote. "I was a total recluse," Carroll said, "just using the landscape." A brief retelling of Carroll's time in Bolinas is included in his book *Forced Entries*, and much of the writing he did while in Bolinas can be found in his *Book of Nods* (Viking, 1986) and the chapbook *Bolinas Poems* (Blue Press, 2010).

In Bolinas Carroll put the finishing touches on *The Basketball Diaries*, his account of being a high-school basketball star, aspiring poet, and serious heroin addict in New York City. The book was published in Bolinas by Michael Wolfe and his Tombouctou Press. An elegant publication, this first edition featured an introduction by Tom Clark (in which an aged, tired Arthur Rimbaud shows up in Bolinas and hangs out with Clark discussing Carroll's book), along with illustrations from a sculpture by Mark

Blane and a cover photo of Carroll by Rosemary Klemfuss—whom Carroll met in Bolinas and later married.

It was also in Bolinas that Carroll began to experiment with writing rock lyrics. In 1978 Patti Smith, his longtime friend from New York, who had already been creating some attention with her Patti Smith Band, invited Carroll to a concert she was to perform at in San Diego. Smith had Carroll come out and, with her band behind him, read some poems. Carroll has said that he was instantly hooked on the energy and immediacy of performing for a rock audience.

Back in Bolinas, Duncan McNaughton turned Carroll on to a local band, a group of long-haired rockers who initially called themselves "Bolinas", but as that was the big taboo, they bowed to local pressure and changed their name to "The Venusians" and then to "Amsterdam". They would later form the nucleus of what would become the Jim Carroll Band.

"The next thing I knew," said McNaughton,"'Jim and the band were appearing at the Mabuhay Gardens in San Francisco."

The Bolinas based performance artist Bill Talen organized the Move Poetry Series at Mabuhay Gardens. Move Poetry was an opportunity for performance artists to find an audience. Talen would often perform, as did Lewis MacAdams, and it was at a Move Poetry performance that Jim Carroll and the band Amsterdam made their first appearance at Mabuhay Gardens.

Carroll left Bolinas in 1979, returning to New York, where he signed a deal with Bantam Books to republish *The Basketball Diaries* (without Tom Clark's introduction), and also landed a recording contract with Rolling Stones Records. His first album was titled *Catholic Boy*.

THINGS COULD HAPPEN
SPONTANEOUSLY

L ewis MacAdams' marriage to Phoebe continued to disintegrate. It was a long, agonizing process, but the outcome was inevitable. By 1974 MacAdams found himself essentially homeless in Bolinas. He stayed with various friends in town but was also spending more and more time in San Francisco where he had landed the position of director of the Poetry Center at San Francisco State University.

One of the temporary homes MacAdams found in Bolinas was in a small shed, which he had helped build a few years earlier. The shed was owned by Bill Niman, who is today a very successful producer of high-quality organic meats. The forty sows that Niman was raising freely roamed in and out of the shed.

The book length poem that MacAdams wrote during this period was *News From Niman Farm*. The final piece in his Bolinas trilogy which started with the journalistic account of the 1971 oil spill, *A Bolinas Report*, and continued with *Tilth*, the eco-political book of interviews with Bolinas farmers. *News From Niman Farm* is a long poem constructed of small poems that build and expand upon one another. The subject matter includes the political concerns that MacAdams was passionately involved with in Bolinas, as well as the sense of loss brought on by the break-up of his marriage. The locale of the poems shifts between Bolinas and San Francisco, just as did MacAdams' life at this time. With lyrics that range from descriptions of the weather, love songs, and the retelling of dreams, *News From Niman Farm* is a dynamic and beautiful work. The final poem, "Calling Coyote Home" is a classic tour de force, wherein the poet encounters the Native American trickster god Coyote Old Man, ultimately interviewing him:

Coyote, are you a Buddhist?
I'm a friend of the Buddhist.
Coyote, what about marriage?
Boy, I'm afraid you're barking up the wrong tree.
It's just the same in your philosophy?
Boy, I don't have no philosophy.
Well, how do you treat women?
I treat everybody good.
You have to,
if you're gonna live in a family,
which I hope you're gonna do
because it's your ass if you don't.

The poem ends with a kind of shape-shifting vision, with the voice of Coyote Old Man fading into that of the poet's:

And coyote actually began to disappear into his own ravings, which began to sound more and more like my own meditations and laments the longer I listened, until the night began to close around me and his yips began to fade, and the only sound was the heater working away and the chorus of frogs and stars.

‡

News From Niman Farm was the first book published by poet Michael Wolfe and his Tombouctou Press. Wolfe, who moved to Bolinas in 1972, is perhaps unique among the poets who came to Bolinas in that he was initially unaware of the poetic community there. Nonetheless, Wolfe fell in quite easily among the poets and in 1974 he bought The Purple Heron Bookstore downtown. He also started the reading series at St. Aiden's Church which became a venue for local and visiting poets. Among the readers featured at St. Aiden's, which was located at the corner of Park and Brighton, were Robert Creeley, Lawrence Kearney, Jim Gustafson, Bobbie Louise Hawkins, John Thorpe, and Jim Carroll.

Sometime in 1975 Lawrence Kearney was hanging out at the Purple Heron and suggested to Wolfe that he start publishing books. "There were so many manuscripts circulating in Bolinas," said

Wolfe, "and I thought it would be great to be able to publish them. Bolinas was a place where things could happen spontaneously." Wolfe applied for and received an NEA grant and Tombouctou Press was born.

Following *News From Niman Farm*, Wolfe published Lawrence Kearney's book *FIVE*, Duncan McNaughton's *Sumeriana*, and *Frenchy & Cuban Pete* by Bobbie Louise Hawkins.

Wolfe did the paste-up for the books himself at his home in Bolinas and contracted with The West Coast Print Center in Berkeley to do the printing and binding. The Tombouctou catalog is impressive and the books themselves were clean, attractive volumes. Wolfe was hired by the Print Center in the late seventies and opened his own bindery shop in west Oakland in 1979. John Thorpe and Lawrence Kearney both worked for Wolfe at the bindery.

Tombouctou ran from 1976 until 1988, which was when Wolfe left Bolinas. His mark upon the Bolinas literary scene was significant. So many important books by Bolinas poets and writers may never have found their way into print without Michael Wolfe and Tombouctou.

‡

In the spring of 1976, *The Bolinas Hearsay News* published an Anniversary Supplement. Printed by Mickey Cummings at the Mesa Press, the Supplement was a community literary magazine, in the spirit of the two magazines that Saroyan and Riviere produced in 1973. Among the stories, poems, and interviews were an excerpt from Orville Schell's book *The Town That Fought to Save Itself*, poetry by Michael Wolfe, Stephen Ratcliffe, and Jim Carroll, and a section (printed on bright yellow paper) of stories and drawings by Bolinas children.

Another community literary effort was a magazine called *Pacific Plate*. Printed "in Bolinas for Bolinas", and featuring a wide range of Bolinas contributors, the first issue starts off with an illustrated description of the Pacific Plate and an essay by local geologist Ralph Camiccia on the 8 major plates on the earth's surface. There are articles on community planning, information on local farming, photographs by Ilka Hartmann, an eco-rage entitled

"Bio-Centennial" by Ponderosa Pine, and a choice selection of poetry and prose.

A non-literary publication that appeared during this time was a little magazine simply entitled *Pamphlet*. Printed by the Bolinas-based Shelter Publications, *Pamphlet* was a progressive source book, the Whole Earth Catalog meets the Farmer's Almanac. It contained recommendations for local farmers, interviews with local old-timers regarding farming, ranching, and gardening, and practical advice on planting cycles in the region.

‡

An active series of readings and concerts were ongoing in Bolinas from the mid to late seventies. Some of these events were held at the Gibson House, a restaurant on Wharf Road. Lewis MacAdams, Bobbie Louise Hawkins, and Aram Saroyan were among those who read there, and local bands such as The Duxbury Reefers and The Venusians also performed at the Gibson House. Readings, concerts and other events were ongoing and well attended at the BPUD as well. Max Crosley's "Ritual" jazz/poetry performances, readings by Bill Berkson, Joanne Kyger, Jim Carroll, and Aram Saroyan, along with benefit performances and readings for the Bolinas School, the *Hearsay News*, and other worthy community institutions and efforts were held at the BPUD.

Among the varied cultural activities that were taking place was a regular informal gathering of the Harrison Dibblee Appreciation Society. Pre-dating the poets in Bolinas during the seventies by 40 years, Marin County poet Harrison Dibblee (1876-1948) was the son of a prominent commission merchant active in San Francisco and the bay area in the 1890s. He was to carry on in the family business and was an important member of the Marin County community in the 1920s and 30s. He also spent a lot of time visiting Bolinas and wrote three books of poetry, all of which carry references to Bolinas—*Hours That Count and Thoughts in Rhyme* (1930), *Calling Quail* (1940), and *The Epic of Bolinas* (1940). Dibblee's grandson, Tom Dibblee, lived in Bolinas in the seventies and took part in the meetings of the Harrison Dibblee Appreciation Society, as did Joanne Kyger and Aram Saroyan. Meetings generally consisted of reading and discussing Harrison Dibblee's poetry. In one of the magazines that Aram Saroyan and Russ Riviere published in Bolinas in 1973, they printed three poems from one of Dibblee's books.

‡

The Turkey Buzzard Review was a unique little magazine that first appeared in July of 1977. With a cover designed by Terry Bell and silkscreened by Arthur Okamura, *The Turkey Buzzard Review* was inspired by Lew Welch's "Song of the Turkey Buzzard" and inside the front cover, above a Susanna Acevedo photograph of two turkey buzzards, was reprinted the last stanza of that poem:

NOT THE BRONZE CASKET BUT THE BRAZEN WING
SOARING FOREVER ABOVE THEE O PERFECT
O SWEETEST WATER O GLORIOUS

WHEELING

BIRD

This first issue, "lovingly dedicated to Lew Welch wherever he may fly", was edited by Dotty LeMieux, assisted by Sara Schrom, Joanne Kyger, Susanna Acevedo, Charles Berrard, Terry Bell, Diana McQuaid, and Michael Rafferty. The magazine featured works by Bill Berkson, Lawrence Kearney, Aram Saroyan, Joanne Kyger, John Thorpe, Michael Wolfe, and Nancy Whitefield, with a collaboration written by Tom Clark and Lewis MacAdams, photographs by Susanna Acevedo, a painting by Lynn O'Hare, and drawings and cartoons by Gordon Baldwin, Terry Bell, Lynn Phillips, and Ted Saladin. Inset among its 24 pages were excerpts from various sources related to turkey buzzards and vultures. The theme set by the Welch poem was carried through the magazine.

Joanne Kyger said, "It was much fun and a group effort. We did have a hilarious theater event presenting 'Woodrat and Gopher visit Tibet', which was a benefit for the second *Turkey Buzzard,* I think. Phoebe got ga-ga and kept kneeling at Lewis' feet, Sara fell over a bench before it was her turn to read, Nancy Whitefield's beanbag chair caught fire, etc., etc. It was a total participatory event, in which the audience acted out as much as the readers-actors."

The Turkey Buzzard Review ran from 1977 to 1981 and produced only four issues, but it was a classic, eclectic little Bolinas magazine.

NOTHING LASTS FOREVER

Even with this ongoing flurry of activity among the poets, there began a slow and steady exodus from Bolinas in the mid-seventies. Everyone had their own reasons, but there was a general shift in the air at the time. The government had tightened up on NEA grants and even welfare money was drying up. It became more and more difficult for poets to get by in Bolinas. Many poets turned to teaching, but living in Bolinas made this problematic—it was a tough commute to San Francisco or Berkeley where there were teaching jobs.

The sixties actually didn't end until the mid-seventies. Bolinas was an outpost of that counterculture movement which was eventually co-opted and devoured by society. Stubbornly holding to those sixties values, Bolinas nevertheless was not immune to the changes in political and economic climate that came about as the seventies progressed.

Robert Creeley spent increasingly more and more time away from Bolinas. This was in part due to teaching and reading gigs everywhere from New York to New Zealand, but also, as Creeley had said, the death of Jack Boyce and his own marital difficulties were contributing factors. Creeley left Bolinas for good in 1976 as his marriage to Bobbie Louise Hawkins finally came to an end.

Gordon Baldwin, who had been the director of the Bolinas Community Center for several years, left town in 1976, moving to Taos. Baldwin remembered that his landlord, Mrs. Sharon, made the comment that he had been renting from her "for a very long time," and it became clear that she had other plans for the property. Reflecting on this, Baldwin decided she was right. He had lived in Bolinas for seven years and he was ready for a change.

Bobbie Louise Hawkins was writing poetry and short prose pieces, the latter exceptionally fine and often humorous reminiscences and accounts of her early life growing up in Texas, and had several books published in the late seventies. She also teamed up with the folk music duo of Rosalie Sorrels and Terry Garthwaite and spent more time away from Bolinas on a series of road trips with Sorrels and Garthwaite performing a blend of folk songs and storytelling.

A newcomer to town in the midst of all those leaving was the writer, Donald Guravich. Originally from Canada, Guravich met Joanne Kyger at the Naropa Institute in Boulder and followed her back to Bolinas in 1978. Living with Kyger, Guravich found work with Bill Brown, eventually learning the art of tree-trimming which he began to do freelance. Guravich edited and published a little series of magazine/chapbooks entitled *No Difference Here* which began in 1980. His terrific little book *Triggers* was published by Tombouctou in 1983.

By the mid-seventies Tom Clark had all but completely withdrawn from the social scene in Bolinas. While he was instrumental in bringing many poets, particularly those from New York, to Bolinas, he never really bought the community line and he held very little respect for what was political consciousness in town. He said that he saw Bolinas as, "a Zippy-the- Pinhead kind of landscape. All individual mutations and variations were condoned because you couldn't be too strange for the place. If you weren't strange you didn't fit in and were resented." In a 1975 interview in the literary journal *Sun & Moon*, Clark said, "My wife says I'm a bitter pastoralist. If so, Bolinas has done this for me."

"Tom was a lot more social in the early days that I lived in Bolinas," said MacAdams. "Most people I knew in Bolinas didn't know Tom at all. He was just this guy they saw jogging early in the morning…I never remember him at any of the poetry readings or anything like that."

Joanne Kyger also said that Clark was only seen jogging, "usually with a grim expression on his face, carrying two big stones, one in each hand, to throw at any dogs that might decide to chase him." Jim Carroll's only reference to Tom Clark in *Forced Entries*, is a fleeting vision of Clark jogging, wearing "one of those Superfly, Back-to-Africa pillbox jobs. He never stops. We seldom speak, but simply nod at each other with a look of camaraderie born of the knowledge that we have both succeeded in our quest to become complete anti-social hermits."

Clark became involved in several journalistic book projects—he wrote a book about the rise and fall of the Oakland Athletics baseball team, and biographies of Damon Runyon and Detroit Tigers pitcher Mark Fidrych. These projects took a lot of time, work and concentration, and contributed to what became his near hermit-like existence in Bolinas. He also produced an impressive amount of poetry during this period as well. In 1978, after ten years on the mesa, the Clarks packed up and moved to Colorado.

Lewis MacAdams left Bolinas in 1979, relocating to Los Angeles. "It got to the point for me," he said, "where I couldn't walk down the road without seeing ghosts. I couldn't go to any corner of the mesa that wasn't overpopulated with images of myself."

‡

The change in the late seventies was in part due to the state of the U.S. economy. In the mid-seventies the OPEC oil crisis caused gasoline prices to skyrocket and inflation took over. It was increasingly difficult to get by financially. Many of the poets had families. In order to keep themselves and their families together, they had to find sources of income—something that wasn't easy to do in Bolinas. Others had simply tired of the scene and the small town "everybody knows what everybody else is up to" atmosphere. As David Meltzer said, "We were in an everyday reality, exoteric and esoteric—many of us were raising families just as a lot of 'beat' folks, in their moment, were—as anyone knows, nothing lasts forever".

The diverse threads or themes that pervade the works written there provide compelling criteria for the distinct character of the place and the community that everyone who lived there was a part of. As for the poets, they each brought with them their unique individual visions, and a convergence of poetries took place. In that convergence, or confluence, it was inevitable that influences would blend.

It's a subtle linkage, as though these were notes toward a poem that was never finished, juxtapositions in a collage-like arrangement working as a cohesive statement, whether that was the intention or not.

‡

A list of the poets, writers and artists who lived for varying periods in Bolinas between 1967 and 1980, gives one a representative sampling of the literary and artistic avant-garde of the time: Paul Alexander, Donald Allen, Gordon Baldwin, Terry Bell, Franco Beltrametti, Bill Berkson, Ted Berrigan, Michael Bond, Ebbe Borregaard, Jack Boyce, Joe Brainard, Richard Brautigan, Jim Brodey, Bill Brown, Jim Carroll, Tom Clark, Robert Creeley, Darrell DeVore, John and Margot Doss, Richard Duerdon, Lew Ellingham, Steve Emerson, Tom Field, Charles Fox, Bob Grenier, Donald Guravich, Jim Gustafson, Paul Harris, Bobbie Louise Hawkins, Dale Herd, Patrick Holland, Lawrence Kearney, Jim Koller, Joanne Kyger, Annie Lamott, Kenneth Lamott, Keith Lampe, Dotty LeMieux, Lewis MacAdams, Duncan McNaughton, Diana Middleton McQuaid, David Meltzer, Alice Notley, Arthur Okamura, Louis Patler, Stephen Ratcliffe, Aram Saroyan, Orville Schell, John Thorpe, Tom Veitch, Lewis Warsh, Peter Warshall, Philip Whalen, Michael Wolfe, and Hanford Woods.

Among the visitors during this period were, John Ashbery, Robert Bly, Andrei Codrescu, Clark Coolidge, Gregory Corso, Edward Dorn, Robert Duncan, Kenward Elmslie, William Everson, Larry Fagin, Lawrence Ferlinghetti, Jane Freilicher, Allen Ginsberg, John Giorno, Philip Guston, R.B. Kitaj, Gerard Malanga, Jeffrey Miller, Pat Nolan, Charles Olson, Tom Raworth, Ed Sanders, Harris Schiff, Gary Snyder, Charlie Vermont, Anne Waldman, and Lew Welch.

Epilogue:
ONWARD

The Indians thought of it [Bolinas] as a healing place, but would not make it a permanent residence. I think I understand that.
    —Aram Saroyan

Aram Saroyan and his family left Bolinas for Ridgefield, Connecticut, in 1984. Bill Berkson held on until 1993, when he relocated to San Francisco where he taught for several years at the San Francisco Art Institute. Bobbie Louise Hawkins left in the early eighties, taking up Anne Waldman on her invitation to teach at the Naropa Institute in Boulder, Colorado. Duncan McNaughton, left, and returned, and left again in the mid-eighties and nineties. He and his wife Genie, still own a house in Bolinas and have plans to move back once again.

In the mid-eighties MacAdams was one of the founding members of Friends of the Los Angeles River, an organization dedicated to saving and restoring the much-maligned L.A. River. It's clear that the environmental activism that he was so deeply invested in during his Bolinas years hadn't left him. He was the Board Chairman of Friends of the Los Angeles River and wrote a long poem about the river and his involvement with it. The first three sections of this poem were published as *The River: Books One, Two and Three* (Blue Press, 2005).

As Lew Welch had written, "It's in your head and hands. Take it anywhere."

Just about every poet that lived there has said that the time they spent in Bolinas was the most magical, crazed, exceptional, and memorable of their lives. "The Bolinas community was a lot of fun," said Bill Berkson, "and very instructive in its own at times confusing manner. Country, rural or ex-urban living was what we all were after and enjoyed as far as each one could."

Duncan McNaughton said, "The fact is, then and now, it is a real town, with the wildest possible permission for the expression of individual need that I have ever seen anywhere."

Poets and poetry continued in Bolinas well after 1980. Poet Joe Safdie edited and published his magazine *Peninsula* there in the late 80s, and Stephen Ratcliffe, who still lives on the mesa, continues to write and publish. Charlie and Marylu Ross, who came to Bolinas via Naropa in the 1980s, published a series of chapbooks under the Smithereens Press imprint, including titles by Berkson, McNaughton, Kyger, Thorpe, Kearney, Bill Brown, Dotty LeMieux, and Magda Cregg.

A July 9, 2000 article in the *New York Times* described Bolinas as "the Howard Hughes of towns." Today the people of Bolinas are still fighting to protect their community and the battle to limit population growth and the construction of new homes on the mesa is ongoing. The incredible increase in property values in Marin County has brought in young professionals who find Bolinas a hip place to buy a house, erect a security fence, and visit on the weekends. Not very popular with the locals, to say the least. A website for surf lessons in Bolinas includes detailed directions and maps to the town. The outside world is again intruding. On a recent visit to Bolinas I saw a bumper sticker on a pickup truck that read, "Why do they call it 'Tourist Season' if you're not allowed to shoot them?"

The values that were formed in the early seventies are still largely adhered to—respect for the natural surroundings and an honest desire to protect this peaceful and beautiful place from uncaring outsiders. *The Hearsay News* still appears three times a week. A walk down Wharf Road can still elicit that hippie vibe. And the sign on Highway 1 is still missing.

The Crystal in Tamalpais

In Tamalpais is a big crystal. An acquaintance told
me the story. A Miwok was giving his grandfather's medicine
bag to the Lowie Museum in Berkeley. He said this man
took him over the mountain Tamalpais, at a certain time
in the year. I believe it was about the time of the
Winter Solstice, because then the tides are really low.
They stopped and gathered a certain plant on the way over
the mountain. On their way to the Bolinas Beach clam patch,
where there is a big rock way out there.

Go out to
the rock. Take out of the medicine bag the crystal
that matches the crystal in Tamalpais. And
                              if your heart is not true
                              if your heart is not true
when you tap the rock in the clam patch
                        a little piece of it will fly off
                        and strike you in the heart
                  and strike you dead.
        And that's the first story I ever heard about Bolinas.

                                        - Joanne Kyger

Photograph accompanying an article entitled "Bolinas Beckons", describing a "vacation fashion field trip" to Bolinas. Clipped from an unknown newspaper from the late 1940s or early 1950s

Muddy road on the mesa, circa 1973

Bill Brown, 1972
Photo by Phoebe MacAdams

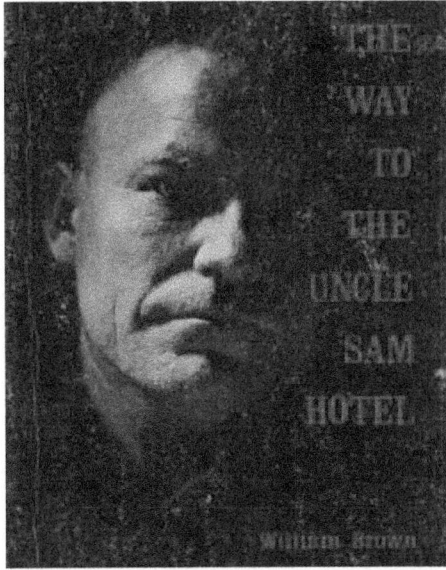

The Way to the Uncle Sam Hotel by William Brown
Coyote Books, 1966
Uncredited cover photo of Bill Brown

Angelica & Tom Clark, 1971

Jack Boyce & Joanne Kyger on the Bolinas mesa, 1969

John Thorpe (Shao), Felicidad & Renee, 1972
Photo by Phoebe MacAdams

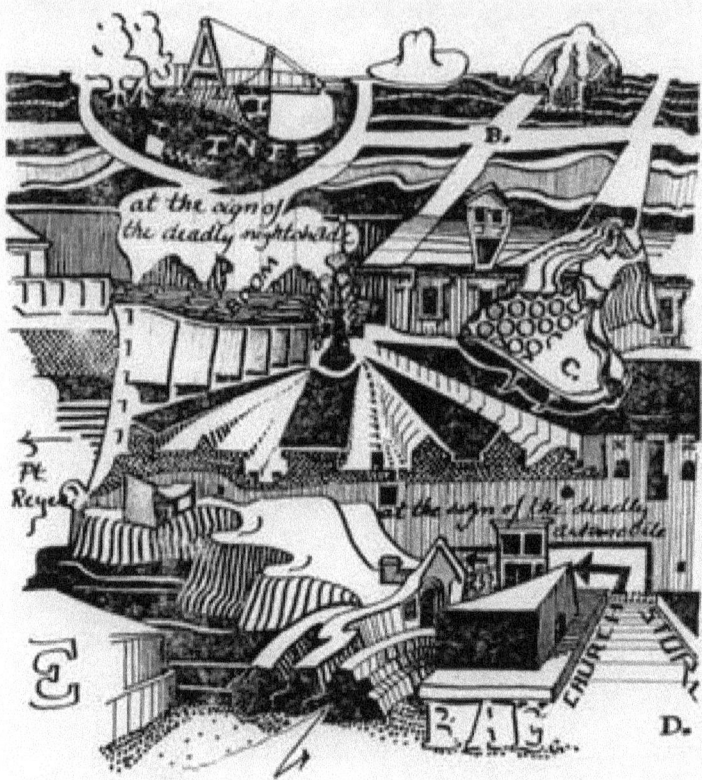

A Map of Bolinas by Gordon Baldwin,
from *The Bolinas Hit*, No. 1, 1969

The Bolinas Hit, No. 1, 1969

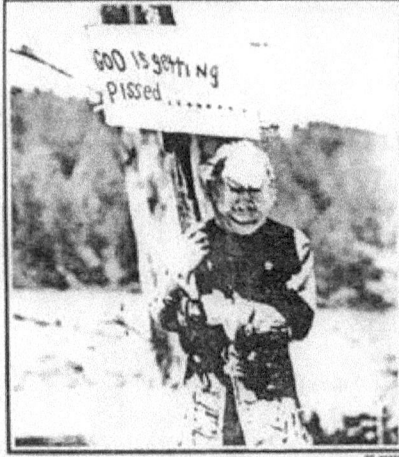

The Bolinas Hit, No. 2, 1969

Part of the Poets Orchestra at Bolinas Community Center, January
1971
Left to right: Tom Veitch, David Meltzer, John Clark (Tom Clark's
brother), Harold Duhl, Ebbe Borregaard

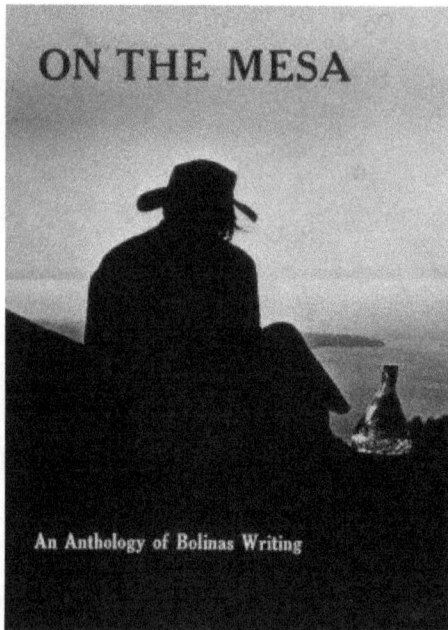

On the Mesa: An Anthology of Bolinas Writing, edited by Joel Weishaus,
City Lights Books, 1971

Berkson and Warsh, photo by Elizabeth Leon Kirkland,1970

Kyger and Codrescu, photo by Elizabeth Leon Kirkland, 1970

Tom and Martha Veitch. 1971

Keith Lampe (aka, Ponderosa Pine), 1972?

Oil Spill, January 1971 - Bolinas lagoon - Boom & hay used as a barrier to keep the oil spill from entering the lagoon

Bags of hay to be used to augment the boom/barrier

Digging up sand for use in sandbags

String of hay bags ready to be deployed

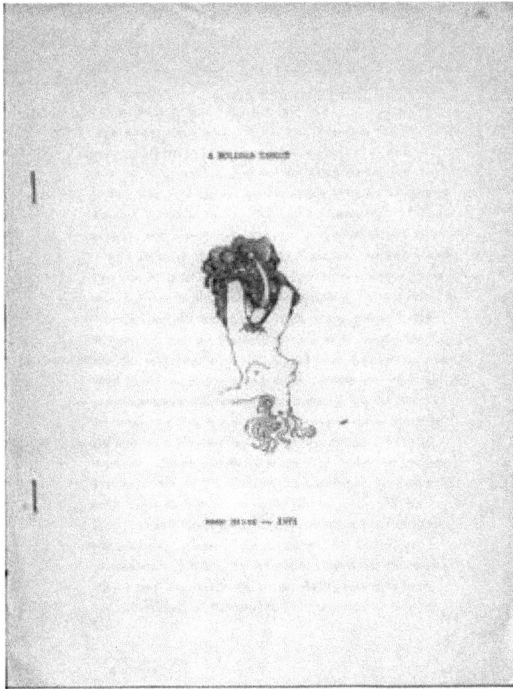

A Bolinas Report, by Lewis MacAdams. Zone Press, Bolinas. 1969

Peter Warshall & Lewis MacAdams, 1972?

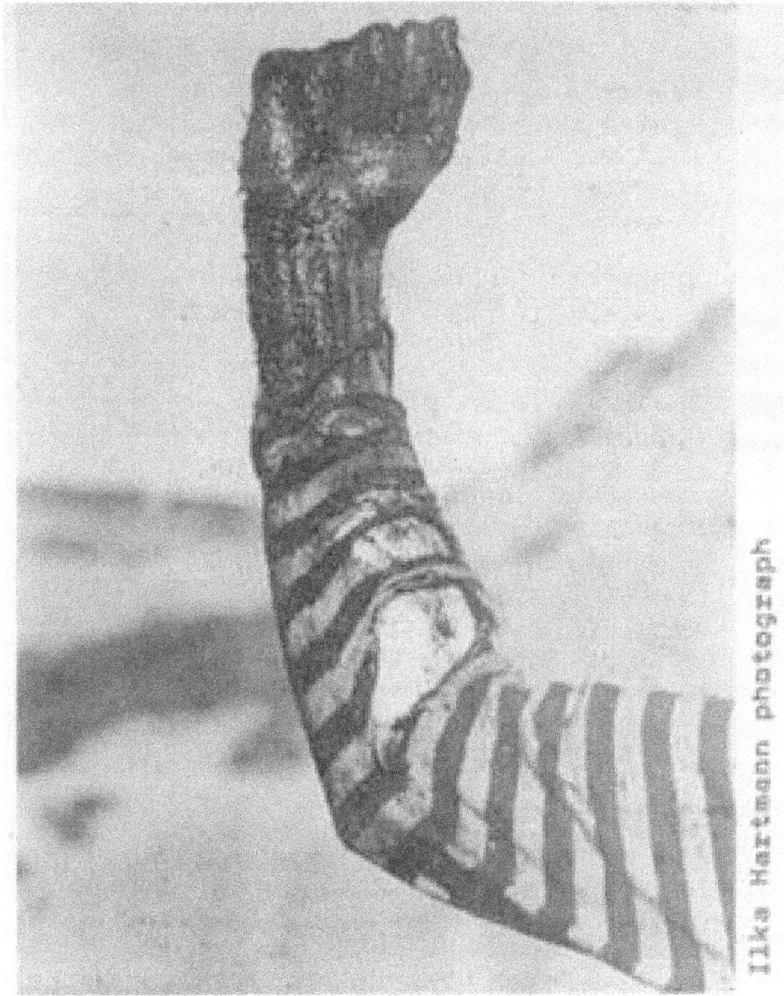

text on image: lest we forget   january 1971   Ilka Hartmann photograph

Ilka Hartmann photo from the first issue of *The Paper*, 1971

The Paper, Issue No. 8. December 12, 1971

Cover of *Bolinas Eyewash* manuscript,
drawn by Ted Berrigan. 1971

First page of "The Creature from the Bolinas Lagoon" by Greg Irons

Joe Brainard in Bolinas, 1971,
photo by Bill Berkson

Scenes of Life at the Capital by Philip Whalen,
Grey Fox, Bolinas, 1971 (Cover photo of Whalen by Ron Sokol)

A Bolinas Journal by Joe Brainard. Big Sky, 1971

Bill Berkson by Joe Brainard (from *A Bolinas Journal*, 1971)

Tilth, by Lewis MacAdams,
Bolinas Future Studies Center, 1972

Lewis MacAdams, photo by Gerard Malanga used on the cover of
Live at the Church, 1977

Toking up - Lewis MacAdams (left) & Tom Clark (right), 1970

Gordon Baldwin's work desk, 1972

Contexts of Poetry: Interviews 1961 - 1971, Four Seasons Foundation, 1973
(Cover shot of Creeley in Bolinas by Gerard Malanga)

Jack Boyce, Joanne Kyger, & Lew Welch in Bolinas, 1969

The Bolinas Book by Aram Saroyan,
cover by Gailyn Saroyan, Other Publications, 1974

Ebbe Borregaard, 1970

Joanne Kyger at Ebbe Borregaard's wedding,
reading "A Testimony for Ebbe and Angela on their Wedding", 1972

Bill Berkson outside Lewis MacAdams' house on the Bolinas mesa,
photo by Phoebe MacAdams. 1972

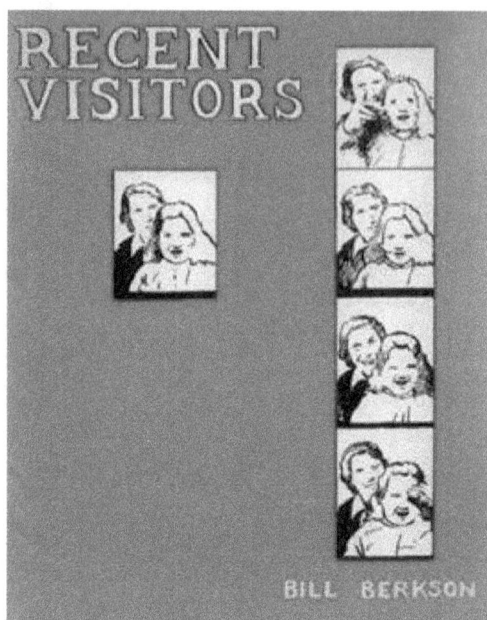

Recent Visitors by Bill Berkson,
Angel Hair Books, 1973

Trip Out & Fall Back by Joanne Kyger,
cover & illustrations by Gordon Baldwin, Arif Press, 1974

Joanne by Joanne Kyger,
cover photo of Kyger by Bill Berkson, Angel Hair Books, 1970

Neil Young by Tom Clark, Angel Hair Books, 1970

Big Sky #1, cover by Greg Irons, 1971

Big Sky #8, cover by Joe Brainard, 1974

Big Sky #10, cover by Gordon Baldwin, 1976

The Cargo Cult by John Thorpe, Big Sky, 1972

Saroyan/Riviere magazine #1,
cover by Arthur Okamura, March 1973

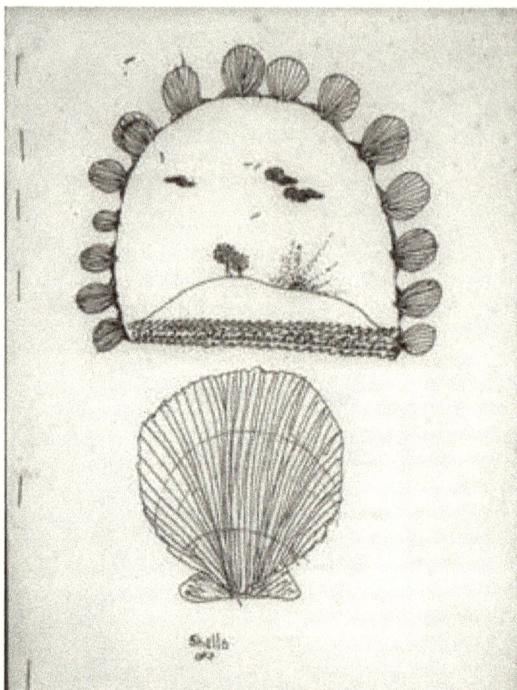

Saroyan/Riviere magazine #2,
cover by Lisa Kleinberg, April 1973

The Bolinas Daily Hearsay News,
First issue, February 30, 1974

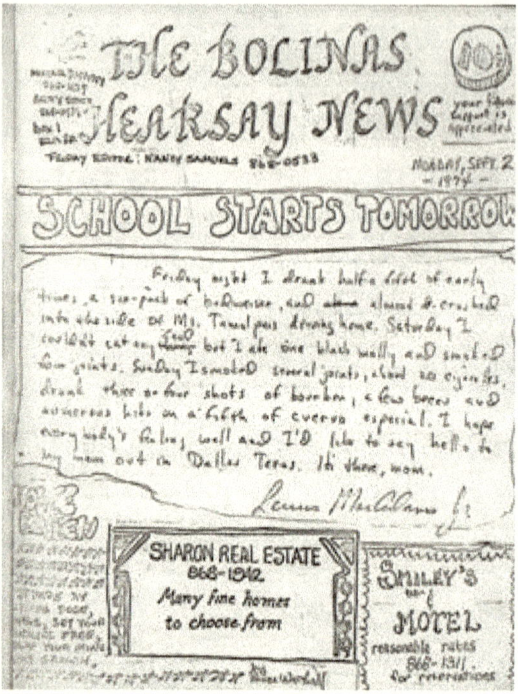

THE BOLINAS HEARSAY NEWS

MONDAY, SEPT. 2
— 1974 —

SCHOOL STARTS TOMORROW

Friday night I drank half a fifth of early times, a six-pack of budweiser, and almost crashed into the side of Mt. Tamalpais driving home. Saturday I couldn't eat any food but I ate one black molly and smoked four joints. Sunday I smoked several joints, about 20 cigarettes, drank three or four shots of bourbon, a few beers and numerous hits on a fifth of cuervo especial. I hope everybody's feeling well and I'd like to say hello to my mom out in Dallas Texas. Hi there, mom.

SHARON REAL ESTATE
868-1942
Many fine homes to choose from

SMILEY'S MOTEL
reasonable rates
868-1311
for reservations

The Bolinas Hearsay News, September 2, 1974

The Bolinas Hearsay News, March 21, 1975

Jim Carroll and Bill Berkson, in Berkson's house on the mesa, 1976

"In watermelon sugar the deeds were
done and done again as my life is
done in watermelon sugar."

In Watermelon Sugar by Richard Brautigan,
Four Seasons Foundation, 1968

Tales of Virtue and Transformation, by Jim Gustafson,
cover drawing by Greg Irons, Big Sky Books, 1974

News from Niman Farm by Lewis MacAdams,
cover photo of Bill & Amy Niman (& hog) by Ilka Hartmann,
Tombouctou, 1976

The Basketball Diaries by Jim Carroll,
cover photo by Rosemary Klemfuss, Tombouctou, 1978

Shit On My Shoes by Duncan McNaughton,
cover photo by Susanna Acevedo, Tombouctou, 1979

The Bolinas Hearsay News Anniversary Supplement, Spring 1976

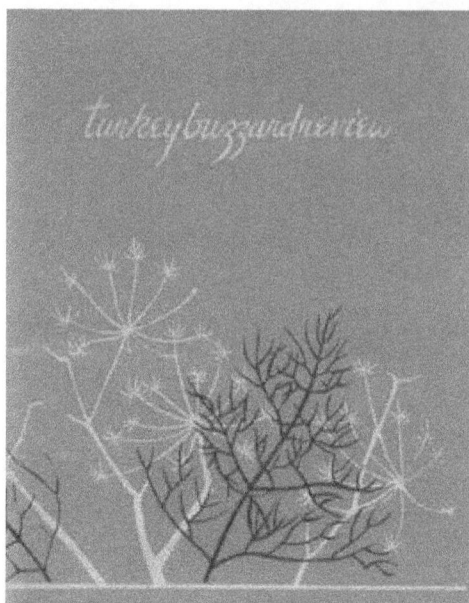

Turkey Buzzard Review, Issue No. 1, 1977,
cover by Terry Bell silkscreened by Arthur Okamura

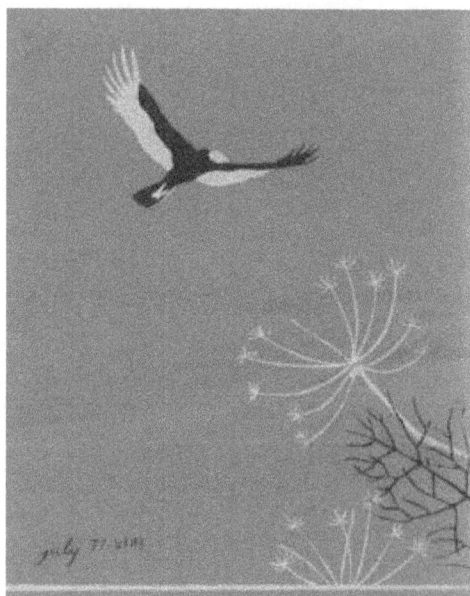

Turkey Buzzard Review, back cover

TERRY GARTHWAITE, BOBBIE LOUISE HAWKINS, ROSALIE SORRELS

Photograph from the *Point Reyes Light* newspaper, 1977

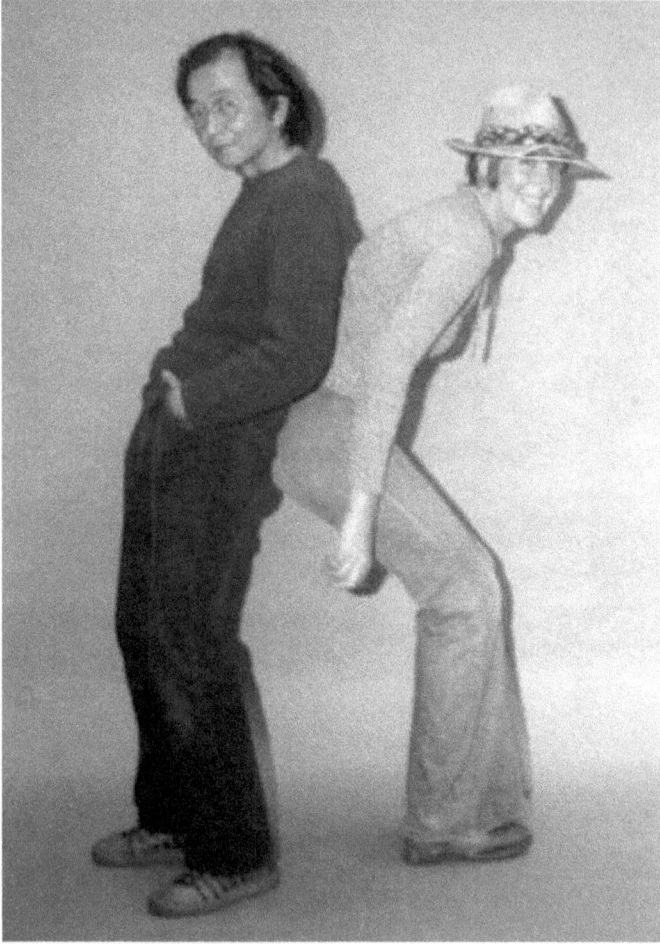

Arthur Okamura and Joanne Kyger, circa 1977,
photograph by Susanna Acevedo

Donald Guravich and Joanne Kyger, 1979,
photograph by Steve Lovi

Peninsula, edited by Joe Safdie, 1988

Donald Guravich & Jim Carroll, circa 1978, photographer unknown

SELECTED BIBLIOGRAPHY

Note: This bibliography is not meant to be a complete listing of every book written in Bolinas from 1967 to 1980. The publications chosen are generally those that are either mentioned or quoted in the text, or publications that I thought best represent Bolinas poetry.

ANTHOLOGY

On the Mesa: An Anthology of Bolinas Writing, edited by Joel Weishaus, City Lights, 1970.

On the Mesa: An Anthology of Bolinas Writing, 50th Anniversary Edition, edited by Ben Estes & Joel Weishaus, The Song Cave, 2021. (Adds several poets that were in or around Bolinas after the original anthology was published in 1970).

PUBLISHED ARTICLES & INTERVIEWS

"Interview with Harrison Dibblee, Jr.", The Carla Ehat Oral History Program, Marin County Free Library, 1975.

"Tom Clark: Inertia and the Highway Patrol", *Sun & Moon,* 1976. Interviewer Pat Nolan.

"Jim Carroll Interview", *San Francisco Review of Books,* June 1980. Interviewer Erik S. McMahon.

"The oil spill that changed West Marin politics", by Joel Reese, *Point Reyes Light,* January 18, 1991.

"Interview with Joanne Kyger", *The Crooked Cucumber,* 9/29/95. Interviewer David Chadwick.

"Anne Waldman: The Early Years…1965-1970", by Joanne Kyger, *Jacket Magazine,* April 2, 2005.

"The Bolinas Poets", *Beat Scene,* Number 51, Late Summer 2006. A large section of this British magazine is devoted to a series of interviews between the editor, Kevin Ring, and former Bolinas poets, including Lewis Warsh, Alice Notley, David Meltzer, Bill Berkson, Lewis MacAdams, Anne Waldman, Tom and Angelica Clark, Duncan McNaughton, and Lawrence Kearney. The section also features short articles on Joanne Kyger and John Thorpe, as well as a reprint of an essay I wrote on Bolinas that first appeared in the webzine *Jack.*

BOLINAS PERIODICALS

The Bolinas Hit: (2 issues) edited by Bill Beckman, Tom Clark and Jim Brodey, 1969.

Sugar Mountain: (1 issue) edited by Lewis Warsh and Tom Clark, 1970.

The Paper: edited by Bill Beckman, 1971-1973

Beaulines: A Diary of Community Consciousness, edited by Bill Beckman, 1973-1974.

Big Sky: edited by Bill Berkson, 1971-1978.

Untitled Bolinas Poetry Magazine: edited by Aram Saroyan and Russ Riviere, 2 issues, 1973.

Hearsay News: published 3 times a week by three separate editorial staffs, 1973-present.

Fathar: edited by Duncan McNaughton. Issues #6, Sept. 1974, and #7, March 1975 were both published in Bolinas.

The Turkey Buzzard Review: edited by Dotty LeMieux, 4 issues published, 1977-1981.

BOOKS

Berkson, Bill:
Recent Visitors, Angel Hair, 1973.
Ants, Arif Press, 1974. With drawings by Greg Irons.
Enigma Variations, Big Sky, 1975.
Blue is the Hero, L Publications, 1976.

Berrigan, Ted & Clark, Tom:
Bolinas Eyewash, unpublished manuscript (a large selection from this manuscript was printed in *GAS: High-Octane Poetry,* Number 3, Summer 1991).

Borregaard, Ebbe:
Sketches For 13 Sonnets, Oyez, 1969.

Brainard, Joe:
Bolinas Journal, Big Sky, 1971.

Brautigan, Richard:
In Watermelon Sugar, Four Seasons Foundation, 1968.

Brown, Bill:
The Way to the Uncle Sam Hotel, Coyote Books, 1967.

Carroll, Jim:
The Basketball Diaries, with an introduction by Tom Clark, Tombouctou, 1978.
The Book of Nods, Penguin, 1986.
Forced Entries, Penguin, 1987.
Bolinas Poems, Blue Press, 2010.

Clark, Tom:
Air, Harper & Row, 1969.
Green, Black Sparrow, 1971.
John's Heart, Goliard/Grossman, 1972.
35, Poltroon Press, 1976.
How I Broke In, Tombouctou, 1977.
When Things Get Tough on Easy Street, Black Sparrow, 1979.

Clarke, John:
Blake, The Institute of Further Studies, Number 7 in the Curriculum of the Soul Series, 1973.

Creeley, Robert:
1.2.3.4.5.6.7.8.9.0, Shambala/Mudra, 1971. drawings by Arthur Okamura.
Thirty Things, Black Sparrow, 1974.
Away, Black Sparrow, 1976.
The Contexts of Poetry: Interviews 1961-1971, Grey Fox, 1976.

Dibblee, Harrison:
Hours That Count and Thoughts in Rhyme, Westward, 1930.
Calling Quail, Kaleidograph Press, 1940.
The Epic of Bolinas, Kaleidograph Press, 1940.

Guravich, Donald:
Triggers, Tombouctou, 1984.
A Brief History of Flying, Sardines Press/Third Ear Press, 2001.
Blue Chips, Blue Press, 2003.
World at Large: Selected Poems 1971-1978, Blue Press, 2011.

Hawkins, Bobbie Louise:
Fifteen Poems, Arif Press, 1974.
Frenchy & Cuban Pete and Other Stories, Tombouctou, 1977.

Herd, Dale:
Early Morning Wind and Other Stories, Four Seasons Foundation, 1972.
Diamonds, Mudra, 1976.
Wild Cherries, Tombouctou, 1980.
Empty Pockets, Coffee House Press, 2015.
Dreamland Court, City Point Press, 2022.

Kearney, Lawrence:
Earthquake, no imprint, 1974.
FIVE, Tombouctou, 1976.

Koller, James:
California Poems, Black Sparrow Press, 1971.
Like It Was, Blackberry Books, 1999.

Kyger, Joanne:
Joanne, Angel Hair Books, 1970.
Places to Go, Black Sparrow Press, 1970.
Trip Out and Fall Back, Arif Press, 1974.
All This Every Day, Big Sky, 1975.
The Wonderful Focus of You, Z Press, 1980.
Just Space, Poems 1979-1989, Black Sparrow, 1991.
About Now: Collected Poems, National Poetry Foundation, 2007.
2012, Blue Press, 2013.

MacAdams, Lewis:
The Bolinas Report, Zone Press, 1971.
Dance, The Institute of Further Studies, Number 16 in the Curriculum of the Soul Series, 1972.
Tilth, Bolinas Future Studies Center, 1972.
News From Niman Farm, Tombouctou, 1976.
Live From the Church, Kulchur, 1977.
The River: Books One, Two & Three, Blue Press, 2005.

MacAdams, Phoebe:
Sunday, Tombouctou, 1983

McNaughton, Duncan:
Dream, The Institute of Further Studies, Number 2 in the Curriculum of the Souls Series, 1973.
A Passage of Saint Devil, Talonbooks, 1976.
Sumerania, Tombouctou, 1977.
Shit On My Shoes, Tombouctou, 1979.

Meltzer, David:
Knots, Tree Books/Christopher's Books, 1971.
Bark: a Polemic, Capra Press, 1973.
Six, Black Sparrow Press, 1976.

Saroyan, Aram:
The Bolinas Book, Other Publications, 1974.
Friends in the World: The Education of a Writer, Coffee House Press, 1992.
Day & Night: Bolinas Poems, Black Sparrow, 1998.

Schell, Orville:
The Town That Fought to Save Itself, Pantheon, 1976.

Thorpe, John:
The Cargo Cult, Big Sky, 1972.
Matter, or giving, Institute of Further Studies, Number 25 in the Curriculum of the Soul Series, 1975.
Exogeny, Trike, 1981.
Five Aces & Independence, Tombouctou, 1981.

Warsh, Lewis:
Long Distance, Ferry Press, 1971.
Part of My History, Coach House Press, 1972.

Warshall, Peter:
Septic Tank Practices, Anchor, 1979. The first edition was published by Mesa Press, Bolinas, with a cover drawn by Arthur Okamura.

Whalen, Philip:
Heavy Breathing, Four Seasons Foundation, 1983. (Collects *Severance Pay, Scenes of Life at the Capital, The Kindness of Strangers,* and *Enough Said*)

Wolfe, Michael:
No, You Wore Red, Tombouctou, 1980.

OTHER SOURCES

Clay, Steven and Phillips, Rodney: *A Secret Location on the Lower East Side, Adventures in Writing, 1960-1980,* The New York Public Library and Granary Books, 1998.

Guthrie, Hammond. *As Ever Was: Memoirs of a Beat Survivor.* SAF Publishing, Ltd., 2002.

Waldman, Anne and Warsh, Lewis. *The Angel Hair Anthology,* Granary Books, 2001.

Bolinas and Stinson Beach (Images of America: California) by The Bolinas Museum and Stinson Beach Historical Society, Arcadia Publishing, 2004.

ACKNOWLEDGEMENTS

Thanks to the poet Micah Ballard who promoted this book to FMSBW and started the ball rolling.

Without the cooperation of the poets who so graciously put up with my pestering questions and so generously provided me with answers and materials ranging from old letters and photographs to fugitive and obscure publications, I could never have attempted or continued in my often wayward and convoluted pursuit of this story.

Heartfelt thanks to Bill Beckman, Bill Berkson, Joe Brainard, Jim Carroll, Tom Clark, John Clarke, Robert Creeley, Donald Guravich, Dale Herd, Joanne Kyger, Lewis MacAdams, Duncan McNaughton, Alice Notley, Aram Saroyan, Tom Veitch, Anne Waldman, Lewis Warsh, Joel Weishaus, Philip Whalen, and Michael Wolfe. Also, to John Thorpe, for talking to me, however briefly, once during a party at Joanne and Donald's house.

Grateful acknowledgement to Richard Schimmelpfeng, Director of Special Collections, Homer Babbidge Library, The University of Connecticut, Frank Walker, Curator, Special Collections, Elmer Holmes Bobst Library, New York University, and Anne Caiger, Manuscripts Librarian, The University Library, UCLA.

I also thank the folks at the Beinecke Rare Book and Manuscript Library at Yale University where most of the source materials, interviews, correspondence, and my early drafts and notes on Bolinas are now archived.

And finally, to Pamela Dewey, who cared when she had no earthly reason to. Maybe I'm amazed.

Kevin Opstedal

Kevin Opstedal, 2020

Kevin Opstedal is the author of over 25 books of poetry including *Dharma Pharmacy & Surf Shop* (Bird & Beckett, 2024), *Ace of Tentacles* (Auguste Press, 2020), and *Pacific Standard Time: New & Selected Poems* (Ugly Duckling Presse, 2016). Born and raised in Venice, CA, Opstedal currently resides in Santa Cruz.

THE DIVERS COLLECTION

Number 1
Hôtel des Étrangers, poems by Joachim Sartorius translated from German by Scott J. Thompson

Number 2
Making Art, a memoir by Mary Julia Klimenko

Number 3
XISLE, a novel by Tamsin Spencer Smith

Number 4
Famous Dogs of the Civil War, a novel by Ben Dunlap

Number 5
Now Let's See What You're Gonna Do, poetry by Katarina Gogou translated from Greek to English by A.S. with an introduction by Jack Hirschman

Number 6
Sunshine Bell / The Autobiography of a Genius, an annotated edition by Ben Dunlap

Number 7
The Profound M: found photos paired with poems by Tamsin Spencer Smith with an introduction by Matt Gonzalez